Cognizable Object in Sa skya Paṇḍita

Artur Przybysławski

Cognizable Object in Sa skya Paṇḍita

An edition and annotated translation of the first chapter of *Tshad ma rigs gter* by Sa skya Paṇḍita and the first chapter of *Tshad ma rigs pa'i gter gyi don gsal bar byed pa* by Go rams pa

Jagiellonian University Press

REVIEWER
dr hab. Cezary Galewicz

COVER DESIGN
Sebastian Wojnowski

With the financial support of the Centre for Comparative Studies of Civilisations of the Jagiellonian University

kagyu translation project

First edition, Kraków 2017

ISBN 978-83-233-4381-3
ISBN 978-83-233-9765-6 (e-book)

JAGIELLONIAN UNIVERSITY PRESS
www.wuj.pl

Jagiellonian University Press
Editorial Offices: Michałowskiego 9/2, 31-126 Kraków
Phone: +48 12 663 23 80, +48 12 663 23 82, Fax: +48 12 663 23 83
Distribution: Phone: +48 12 631 01 97, Fax: +48 12 631 01 98
Cell Phone: +48 506 006 674, e-mail: sprzedaz@wuj.pl
Bank: PEKAO SA, IBAN PL 80 1240 4722 1111 0000 4856 3325

TABLE OF CONTENTS

NOTE ON BIBLIOGRAPHIC SOURCES AND ACKNOWLEDGMENTS

Part II of this book – translation and edition of Go rams pa's text – was originally published in *Journal of Indian Philosophy* as

- Cognizable Object in *Tshad ma rigs gter* According to Go rams pa, *Journal of Indian Philosophy*, 44 (2016): 957–991.

Some parts of the introduction of this publication are included into the Introduction below. The text of the translation was slightly modified.

My thanks go to Ācārya Bhuchung Dorla Nupa (Choying Tendar) for his invaluable help with translation; to Professor Kenneth Maly and Dr. Julian Schott for all their remarks and suggestions; to Lucy Ralph for her editorial help and to – last but not least – Professor Marta Kudelska for her constant support.

INTRODUCTION

Sa skya Paṇḍita's *Tshad ma rigs gter* shares the quality of works like Plotinus' *Enneads*, being very faithful to the tradition and yet breaking through. Plotinus humbly considered himself only a commentator of Plato, while at the same time he opened the new era of Neoplatonism in Greek thought – genuine and inventive, discovering new themes for philosophical reflection. Similarly, Sa skya Paṇḍita aimed simply at a faithful explanation of Dignāga's and Dharmakīrti's views. As he said at the beginning of his most fundamental treatise in Tibetan epistemology:

> Among the proponents of theories of true cognitions there are some who fail to notice wrong conceptions. So this [text] was composed in order to disprove them and to proclaim the real meaning.[1]

Nevertheless this double task of correcting the faults of former reception of Buddhist epistemology in Tibet and restoring Dignāga's and Dharmakīrti's philosophy to its original form led him to the most original and characteristically Tibetan exposition of the *pramāṇa* system. Like Immanuel Kant's *Critique of Pure Reason* with its revolutionary rethinking of classical metaphysics, *Tshad ma rigs gter* was both a critical assessment of Tibetan forefathers and the establishing a new more idealistic tradition in epistemology by way of a close reading of these Indian classics. As Leonard W.J. van der Kuijp claims:

> These works [*Tshad ma rigs gter* and its autocommentary] constitute, in fact, the very first attempt, whether in India, Tibet, China, Japan, or Mongolia, at making sense out of the huge corpus of logical works written by his Indian precursors. The

[1] See p. 31 below.

> sheer intellectual power that vibrates behind this undertaking can only astound one, and once again points to the genius of this man.[2]

Matthew Kapstein rightly says that *Tshad ma rigs gter* "was to be one of the most widely studied philosophical works ever composed by a Tibetan author."[3] But this is not so much the case in Western research on Tibetan *pramāṇa*. Despite its rank and significance *Tshad ma rigs gter* initially attracted relatively little attention from the scholars, even the ones dealing extensively with Sa skya Paṇḍita like David P. Jackson or Jonathan C. Gold.[4] In both cases it is the *mkhas pa 'jug pa'i sgo*, a significant but philosophically much less important treatise, that was chosen as the object of inquiry.[5] When David P. Jackson in 1987 did a review of previous research on *Tshad ma rigs gter*, it took only two and a half pages to list just a few references to this work in texts dealing actually with other topics. The only exception to this was one paper of van der Kuijp, devoted entirely to *Tshad ma rigs gter* itself.[6] In the subsequent years up to 2007, around twenty texts on *Tshad ma rigs gter* were published. The whole western research on *Tshad ma rigs gter* before 2007[7] was summarized by Pascale Hugon in her *Trésors du*

---

[2] Van der Kuijp (1983: 101).

[3] Kapstein (2000: 89).

[4] Cf. Jackson (1987) and Gold (2007). These two books are quite complimentary since the focus of the first one is the third chapter of *mkhas pa 'jug pa'i sgo*, while the second one deals with first two chapters. Jackson does address *Tshad ma rigs gter* in his book but in a very general way. Cf. also Jackson (1995).

[5] Except the two above mentioned books. Cf. also Verhagen (2005).

[6] Cf. van der Kuijp (1979). Four years later, with the publication of *Contributions to the Development of Tibetan Buddhist Epistemology* by van der Kuijp, Western scholarship for the first time engaged more extensively in the research on *Tshad ma rigs gter*. The author of this fundamental work with his intention of introducing *Tshad ma rigs gter* to a wider audience offered both an assessment of Sa skya Paṇḍita's position within Tibetan epistemological tradition and the first translation of *Tshad ma rigs gter* fragments. Pioneering in the field of studies on Tibetan *pramāṇa*, the work of van der Kuijp thus became the first serious step towards reception of Sa skya Paṇḍita's epistemology in the West (cf. also van der Kuijp (1993a) and van der Kuijp (1993b)). One year later Zoltán Horváth published a general outline of *Tshad ma rigs gter* (Horváth 1984).

[7] The first serious assessment and analysis of concrete philosophical ideas upheld by Sa skya Paṇḍita can be found in *Recognizing Reality. Dharmakīrti's Philosophy and its Tibetan Interpretations* by Georges B.J Dreyfus, published in 1997. The author extensively addresses quite a few important notions of Sa skya Paṇḍita's system (e.g., universals and mental states), showing them in the wider context of Tibetan philosophical debates that took place mainly between the dge lugs and Sa skya traditions. Even though the book gives priority to dge lugs epistemology, it still remains one of the most penetrating elaborations on the philosophical issues that inhere in the *Tshad ma rigs gter*.

Concerning Sa skya Paṇḍita theory of inference the texts by Tillemans are of crucial importance. The subtitle of his excellent *Scripture, Logic, Language* by Tillemans (1999) – *Essays on Dharmakīrti and his Tibetan Successors* – leads one to expect some larger comments on Sa skya Paṇḍita. But unfortunately, except for three pages of analysis of his opinion on *sapakṣa* (Tillemans 1999: 90–92), he is only mentioned a few times. Nevertheless his later text "On *sapakṣa*," with

raisonnement. Sa skya Paṇḍita et ses prédécesseurs tibétains sur les modes de fonctionnement de la pensée et le fondement de l'inférence.[8] Her monumental two volume book in turn became a new milestone in this field and most extensive study on *Tshad ma rigs gter*. The first volume is actually the first monograph of Sa skya Paṇḍita's epistemology covering the historical context of his philosophy focusing on the influence of rNgog Blo ldan shes rab, gTsang nag pa brTson 'grus seng ge, mTshur ston gZhon nu seng ge,[9] and in particular of course Phya pa Chos kyi seng ge. The main focus of the book is the problem of inference discussed in a very wide context – both historical and philosophical (typology of cognizable objects, types of cognition, *apoha*, *trairūpya*). The second volume contains the first translation into a European language (French) of the fourth chapter and part of the tenth chapter of *Tshad ma rigs gter*.

In 2010 Bruce J. Stewart published the text analyzing the notion of direct perception in *Tshad ma rigs gter* based heavily on the commentary on Go rams pa (it contains some remarks on cognizable object, mainly on "object associated with words [*sgra don*][10]").[11] The latest contribution to the research on *Tshad ma rigs gter* is the text "Sa skya Paṇḍita's Anti-realism as a Return to the Mainstream" by Jonathan C. Gold (2014). The author analyzes Sa skya Paṇḍita's philosophy of language, showing the crucial role of karmic tendencies in a linguistic model of reference.

This book is another small step on the path of reception and study on *Tshad ma rigs gter* in the West and deals with Sa skya Paṇḍita's theory of cognizable object presented in the first chapter of his *opus magnum*.

---

some introductory analysis of the chapter on inference-for-oneself in *Tshad ma rigs gter*, became the point of departure for more extensive research on the *trairūpya* doctrine in Sa skya Paṇḍita, presented in his "The slow death of the *trairūpya* in Buddhist logic. A propos of Sa skya Paṇḍita." This text, together with a complementary article "Interpretations of the *trairūpya* in Tibet" by Hugon, offers an insightful analysis of this key concept in Buddhist epistemology in Sa skya Paṇḍita in its complex reference both to Indian sources and Phya pa Chos kyi seng ge's view.

[8] Cf. Hugon (2008: 107–109).

[9] Cf. also Hugon (2004). In Hugon (2002) one can also find research on the basic framework of Sa skya logic as formulated by one of the most prominent commentators of Sa skya Paṇḍita – Glo bo mkhan chen bSod nams lhun grub – together with French translation of his rtags rigs treatise.

[10] Concerning *sgra don* cf. Dreyfus (1997: 221–222, 251).

[11] He is also the author of the doctoral dissertation *A Translation of and Introduction to the* "Direct Perception" *chapter of Go-rams-pa's* sde bdun mdo daṅ bcas pa'i dgoṅs pa phyin ci ma log par 'grel pa tshad ma rigs pa'i gter gyi gsal bar byed pa, submitted in 1983 (Columbia University).

Cognizable Object in *Tshad ma rigs gter* – introductory remarks

The first chapter of *Tshad ma rigs gter* – translated below with the commentary of Go rams pa – is an analysis of cognizable object. It starts with the definition of what is cognizable as: "Definition of the object: that which is knowable by mind."[12] This very short definition is explained by Go rams pa as follows:

> Definition of the object: that which is knowable by mind. Definition of the cognizable [*shes bya*] having equal scope is that which can be made into an object of mind. Definition of the perceptible [*gzhal bya*] is that which is to be realized by valid cognition. Definition of the established basis [*gzhi grub*] is that which is observed by valid cognition. Definition of really existent [*yod nges*] is that which can be seen by valid cognition.[13]

After slight rewording Sa skya Paṇḍita's formula in the first sentence,[14] Go rams pa provides a useful list of synonyms, all of which describe the cognizable object in terms of perception, thus cutting off all possible doubts concerning the scope of the listed terms. The object is always something that is cognized, realized, observed, seen, known by the mind or valid cognition and seems to be defined solely in terms the cognitive process operating on it. Even though Go rams pa does not talk about the object apart from cognizing it, it does not mean that here the philosophical position behind it is idealism. Sa skya Paṇḍita's view – following closely Dharmakīrti – is based to a large extent on the Sautrāntika realistic system, which did not claim that the perceived object is in any way constructed in the act of perception itself.[15] Simply, for Buddhist philosophers there is no sense in talking about the object apart from the perception that confirms its existence and this approach comes from the generally realistic attitude of Indian philosophy that proper cognition has to have a real object and cannot grasp an unreal entity.

After introducing the subject of the first chapter, Sa skya Paṇḍita starts discussing it in the context of fourfold division of cognizable object introduced by Tibetan philosophers in the process of inventive assimilation of Dharmakīrti's system. As Śākya mchog ldan says:

---

[12] See p. 39 below.

[13] See p. 113 below.

[14] The difference is, in fact, of minor importance. Instead of agentive *blos* there is possessive *blo'i*. Later on at the very beginning of second chapter Sa skya Paṇḍita repeats the definition of cognizable object with a possessive construction.

[15] Cf. Dreyfus (1997: 76–79), Dhammajoti (2007: 41–43). Cf. also Dunne (2004: 65–79).

> If to analyze the object, what comes from the scriptures is apprehended object and object of engagement. Concerning the conventions introduced by early Tibetans, there are appearing object and conceived object.[16]

The theory of the object formulated by Dharmakīrti, who distinguished only two types of the cognizable object,[17] was reinterpreted by Phya pa chos kyi seng ge adjusting it to his strongly realistic approach. Struggling with the problem of the relation between reality and concept (object universal), which was held to be unreal by Dharmakīrti, thus making it difficult to explain how the thought can apprehend real object, he introduced two additional types of objects of cognition to build the bridge between conceptual cognition and real objects it is supposed to reveal.

According to this fourfold typology, the real object of direct perception is classified as appearing object, apprehended object and object of engagement, since the way it appears is the way it is apprehended being thus accessible as an object of practical engagement. In case of conceptual cognition an outer, really existing object is not the object that appears to it. What appears to it is object universal, a concept through which the former one can be apprehended (as apprehended object) and conceptualized (as conceived object) and finally becoming the subject of activity (as object of engagement).[18]

This daring emendation of Dharmakīrti's system became an important issue that divided Tibetan philosophers. Even though some couldn't accept it, the terminology introduced by Phya pa influenced the whole Tibetan epistemological tradition. For example, mTshur ston gzhon nu seng ge, Sa skya Paṇḍita's teacher,[19] accepts only the following threefold division of the cognizable object:

> Generally there are three [types] of cognizable object, namely apprehended object, conceived object, object of engagement.[20]

Sa skya Paṇḍita assumes a fourfold division as his point of departure for questioning it, after analyzing the problems triggered by it. Thus he begins classically with a refutation of others systems and what is meant by them is of course the

[16] S 296 [*yul la dbye na/ gzhung las 'byung ba ni/ gzung ba'i yul dang/ 'jug pa'i yul lo/ bod snga mas tha snyad byas pa ni/ snang yul dang zhen yul lo/*].

[17] Cf. van Bijlert (1989: 55–58).

[18] For more on Phya pa's typology of object, cf. Dreyfus (1997: 379–383), Hugon (2008: 137–159).

[19] Concerning his influence on *Tshad ma rigs gter* cf. Hugon (2004: xii–xv).

[20] Hugon (2004: 4) [*spyir shes pa'i yul la gsum ste/ gzung yul dang/ zhen yul dang/ 'jug yul lo//*]. Go rams pa in his commentary translated here lists cognizable objects in the same order as mTshur ston gzhon nu seng ge adding at the beginning the fourth one: the appearing object [*snang yul*] that was ignored in the first chapter on the object of cognition in *sGron ma*.

tradition of Phya pa chos kyi seng ge and his followers addressed in the text as "some Tibetans." Sa skya Paṇḍita starts with discussing the status of dubious objects: object universal grasped in conceptual cognition and nonexistent clearly appearing, which is grasped by reverse nonconceptual cognition. Before discussing the status of these objects, one has to clarify the notion of reverse nonconceptual cognition [*rtog med log shes*].

Reverse nonconceptual cognition is the type of erroneous cognition defined as follows in *Tshad ma rigs gter*:

> definition of reverse cognition: apprehension of something invalidated by something that is not [that what was to be apprehended].[21]

The so called reverse cognition in the *Tshad ma rigs gter* is classified as non-cognizing state of mind, so actually it is not cognition in the proper sense. It does not apprehend the object that it seems to apprehend, it grasps something else, and that is why it is reverse cognition or even the opposite of cognition. Actually, in the case of reverse cognition, there is no proper cognition being harmed in this way or another but rather proper valid cognition is simply replaced with invalid perception. As 'Jam dbyangs blo gter dbang po says in his commentary to the *Tshad ma rigs gter*:

> Definition of reverse cognition: it is the apprehension of the object in such a way that it is the state of mind which is invalidated by other valid cognition [cognizing] that it is not that [object but] it is something else.[22]

Thus reverse cognition is not just the wrong apprehension of the object that is given in valid cognition as well. Rather it is wrong perception because it completely misses the object and grasps something else.

Generally there are two types of that cognition – conceptual and non-conceptual. Go rams pa gives the following classification of them:

> There are three conceptual reverse cognitions: the erroneous one concerning shape, like apprehending a multicolored rope as a snake; the erroneous one concerning time, like apprehending a present blue color as the blue color from the past; the

---

[21] T1 84 [*log rtog gi mtshan nyid ni/ de 'dzin pa de min gyis/ gnod pa*].

[22] *Tshad ma rigs gter gyi mtshan 'grel sde bdun gsal ba'i sgron me* (*The Commentary on Treasury of Epistemology that is The Torch Elucidating Seven Treatises*), in: TRC 377 [*yul de nyid du 'dzin pa la de min pa gzhan yin pa'i tshad ma gzhag gyis gnod pa yod pa'i blo ni log shes kyi mtshan nyid*].

erroneous one concerning the object, like apprehending aloe tree and juniper tree as one type.

There are two non-conceptual reverse cognitions: the error of sense consciousness, like a sense consciousness seeing two moons; and the error of mental consciousness, like the consciousness of seeing clearly the dream.[23]

In case of both types of non-conceptual reverse cognition, what is perceived does not exist at all, even though it does somehow arise within the field perception.[24] Hence the name "nonexistent clearly appearing" in case of non-conceptual perception.

Sa skya Paṇḍita aims at showing that in the case of non-conceptual reverse cognition the so called nonexistent clearly appearing cannot be considered an apprehended object,[25] since an apprehended object is in fact an outer entity that is given to the subject either directly or indirectly by way of its aspects.[26] The illusion of two moons, seen after pressing the eyeballs, or dreaming does not exist on the outside. Thus they are not apprehended by the subject in the way that the real tree is apprehended. But still there is something that is given in cognition, something within the field of perception that is taken to be two moons, that looks like two moons. This is called the appearing object by Phya pa's tradition, which in this way reifies illusion despite its dubious status making it into an object of cognition, another point with which Sa skya Paṇḍita cannot agree.

In the case of conceptual reverse cognition, there is something to play the role of apprehended object – a rope mistakenly taken to be a snake which is the appearing object.[27] The error here is just wrong conceptualization by which the

---

[23] G 54 [*rtog pa dang rtog med log shes gnyis las/ dang po ni/ thag khra la sbrul du 'dzin pa lta bu rnam pa la 'khrul ba dang / da ltar gyi sngon po la 'das pa'i sngon por 'dzin pa lta bu dus 'khrul pa dang / sha pa dang shug pa gnyis rigs gcig tu 'dzin pa lta bu yul la 'khrul pa dang gsum mo// rtog med log shes la/ zla ba gnyis snang gi dbang shes lta bu dbang shes 'khrul pa dang/ rmi lam gsal snang gi shes pa lta bu yid shes 'khrul pa gnyis yod do//*].

[24] This is also the case even when the type of the tree is mistakenly identified or when a white conch is perceived as yellow because of jaundice (the example used by Sa skya Paṇḍita). Cf. discussion of this issue in Stoltz (2006: 574–577).

[25] In his synopsis of Sa skya Paṇḍita's rejection of Phya pa's approach, Go rams pa points out exactly this mistake of identifying appearing object with apprehended object as crucial point discussed in *Tshad ma rigs gter*. Cf. Go rams pa's commentary below.

[26] This was exactly the Sautrāntika view questioned by Phya pa who insisted on the fact that appearing object and conceived object must be the same because then there is no question of the aspect rather obscuring the real outer object than revealing it since there is no way to verify the convergence of the object and its aspect when the subject perceives only aspects. More on Sautrāntika view in Sa skya Paṇḍita cf. Hugon (2008: 161–165).

[27] As Dreyfus explains: "The appearing object of a conception (*rtog pa'i snang yul*), understood in a technical sense, is necessarily unreal. It must be distinguished from the real object that appears to

concept – or the so called object universal – of the snake is taken to be an outer object. Non-conceptual reverse cognition cannot be explained in that way, since there is no concept involved that could serve as an explanation for an erroneous experience that simply results from wrong interpretation. There is only what appears while there is nothing that could be apprehended correctly. Determining the status of this kind of perceptual illusions was not an easy task for Buddhist philosophers, and the text of Sa skya Paṇḍita under discussion here remains ambiguous. As we can see in the commentary translated below, Go rams pa himself admits that he is not certain what the original view of the *Tshad ma rigs gter* is – on the one hand he claims that non-conceptual erroneous cognition does not have an appearing object and on the other hand he claims that the nonexistent that clearly appears, as the object of non-conceptual erroneous cognition, is an appearing object. The reason for this hesitation is a very general statement of Sa skya Paṇḍita himself, who, in discussing the status of nonexistent clearly appearing and object universal, used the general term "the object" without specifying which of the four he actually meant. In any case what both have in common is the fact that what appears within the field of cognition does not represent the outer object: the object universal as a concept of the snake does not represent any real snake (or the rope mistaken as a snake) and a dreamt object does not represent any really existing outer object. Sa skya Paṇḍita succeeds in refuting the idea that a nonexistent clearly appearing cannot be an object of direct perception, since in that case appearing object, apprehended object and object of engagement are just one and the same. Thus if direct perception has an object, it cannot be erroneous. But still his explanation can be considered insufficient because he does not explain how non-conceptual erroneous cognition takes place nor what is given in it.[28] This was exactly what Phya pa tried to do, claiming, as Śākya mchog ldan explains, that "there are three apprehended objects: an object which is particular, an object universal and nonexistent clearly [appearing]."[29] Of course a nonexistent clearly appearing cannot be the object of engagement, so the only

---

that conception (*yul de nog pa la snang ba*). Accordingly, ajar, for example, appears to a conceptual cognition but is not its appearing object, which is the object universal of the jar. This artificial distinction is made to conciliate the Ge-luk view of thought and language as partially reflecting reality with Dharmakīrti's assertion that thought does not take real things as its objects of comprehension (*meya, gzhal bya*). According to this interpretation, Dharmakīrti did not intend to exclude that real things appear to thought but only that they are their appearing objects in the technical sense of the word. Only object universals are the appearing objects of conceptual thought. Real entities are not appearing objects of thought even though they appear to it." Dreyfus (1997: 323).

[28] It the twelfth root stanza of first chapter and auto-commentary he only calls non-conceptual erroneous cognition an appearance (*snang ba*) and says that it is mind or cognition itself.

[29] S1, II.3.5–4.3 [*gzung yul gsum ste/ don rang gi mtshan nyid dang/ don spyi dang med pa gsal ba'o/*].

possibility of error would be that in the case of nonconceptual erroneous cognition a nonexistent clearly appearing is only one of the two: either appearing object or apprehended object. If, for example, two moons are given in that perception, are they then appearing object or apprehended object? If they are apprehended object, what is appearing object? If they are appearing object, what is apprehended object? This kind of questions that arise when analyzing Phya pa's typology of objects cannot be answered since, as was said above, in the case of nonconceptual cognition appearing object, apprehended object and object of engagement are one and the same. Thus Sa skya Paṇḍita's critique of Phya pa's typology of cognizable objects is sound and in accordance with Dharmakīrti (PV III 64 cd) and the answer to the question how erroneous nonconceptual cognition comes about can be found not in *Tshad ma rigs gter* but in Dharmakīrti himself and is summarized by Dunne as follows:

> from one perspective, certain entities are *not* ultimately real, but from another perspective, the same entities *are* ultimately real. In the case of the 'hair' seen with the cataractous eye, Dharmakīrti notes that it appears vividly precisely because, even though wrongly interpreted as 'hair,' *the image itself is still a mental event*, and as such, *the image* (not its cause) is a mental particular. But when construed as the perception of an external object that has the causal characteristics expected of hair, the image is *not* a particular. What is important about this technique is that Dharmakīrti also applies it to conceptually construed universals. Construed as entities that are instantiated in multiple particulars, they are not ultimately real. But construed as mental events, they *are* ultimately real.[30]

Thus the crucial thing in solving this kind of problems is a precise typology of cognizable objects. And one of the advantages of Go rams pa's commentary is its very clear presentation of all possible divisions of cognizable object presupposed in *Tshad ma rigs gter* which are the basis for refuting objections addressing Sa skya Paṇḍita's view. The divisions are the following:

- Division into four objects from the point of view of the way of making into an object;
- Division into two truths from the point of view of the nature;
- Division into direct and indirect from the point of view of the object of engagement;
- Division into two, the particular and the universal, from the point of view of the way of engagement.

[30] Dunne (2004: 90).

The doubts concerning the status of a given object and the ensuing problems usually arise from mixing divisions. Thus for example, Sa skya Paṇḍita confronted serious objection when insisting ultimately on the fact that there is only one cognizable object, contradicting Dignāga, who claimed that there are the two, namely the particular in the case of direct perception and the universal in the case of inference. [31] Explaining Sa skya Paṇḍita's view of this matter, Go rams pa refers to his clear divisions of the cognizable objects that he just introduced: "there are the two posited – particular and universal – since there are two ways of comprehending: from the point of view of the own nature only the particular is comprehended, whereas the other is comprehended from the point of view of the object universal."[32] Since there are two ways of cognizing, there are accordingly two cognizable objects. But this does not mean that from the point of view of the object in itself there are two different types. Because in the end valid cognition reveals only one type of object – the particular existing independently outside, and this fact is taken for granted together with Sautrāntika realism mentioned above. As Go rams pa explains:

> it is shown that it is cognition that becomes the cause for adopting and rejecting the objects that can bring benefit and harm. In this way the object that can bring benefit and is to be adopted by valid cognition and the object that can bring harm and is to be abandoned are exclusively the particular, since what is exclusively particular can bring benefit and harm while the universal cannot do this.[33]

Dignāga says "*mtshan nyid gnyis gzhal bya*"[34] – the two characteristics--entities [*mtshan nyid*], namely particular [*svalakṣaṇa*, *rang mtshan*] and universal [*sāmānyalakṣaṇa*, *spyi mtshan*] are the one and only object: the perceptible [*gzhal bya*]. Thus the perceptible analyzed from the point of view of cognition is two-fold. But analyzed as an object in itself it is only one, namely the particular. Even

---

[31] Dignāga's theory of object of cognition, cf. Chu (2006). As Dreyfus points out, the controversy was actually stimulated by the ambiguous position of the forefathers of Tibetan epistemology and Sa skya Paṇḍita's position is "not without support in Dharmakīrti's writings. In discussing valid cognition, Dharmakīrti asserts that nondeceptiveness (*avisamvādanam*, *mi slu ba*), the defining characteristic of valid cognition, consists of the capacity to perform a function in accordance with the way it is cognized by that cognition. Only causally effective phenomena (*vastu*, *dngos po*) have such a capacity. So, valid cognitions are nondeceptive inasmuch as they relate appropriately to real things (*svalakṣaṇa*, *rang mtshan*). Therefore, the conclusion that only real, that is, specifically characterized phenomena are objects of valid cognitions is hard to resist." Dreyfus (1997: 78).

[32] See p. 135 below.

[33] See p. 131 below.

[34] PS I 2b.

the universal as mental event, despite the fact of being general representation, at the very moment of taking place in the mind is particular. That is why it can be effective as a means of obtaining the outer object. This is also the case with the subcategory of *spyi mtshan*[35] that is object universal,[36] which triggered so much discussion. The object universal is thus related both to the singular object that is represented by it and also to the universal. As a manifestation in the mind or, to put it more precisely, as the act of cognizing mind, object universal has its particular moment, since it is just a singular act or mental event. At the same time it has its general moment, since it is referred to as universal, which is its conceptual content. Thus the object universal is triggered in the mind by a particular, but what it does is to establish or grasp a universal. These two aspects make the object universal different from the nonexistent clearly appearing. This is clearly stated by Go rams pa:

> concerning the first one [the object universal], even though it is not a particular, on the basis of it the object of engagement, which is the particular, is obtained, and concerning the second one [nonexistent clearly appearing] its own nature is not the particular and [therefore] on the basis of it object of engagement, which is the particular, is not obtained at all.[37]

It is worth noticing that Go rams pa insists on the fact that in its nature a non-existent clearly appearing is not any particular while, talking about the object universal, he does not refer to its nature – probably because he felt that it is not so clear or at least ambiguous, as I pointed out above.[38] Nevertheless the difference

---

[35] As Go rams pa puts it, the universal "is comprehended from the point of view of the object universal," p. 135 below, and gives the following definition of universal: "imputation seen as the common one [*thun mong bar snang ba'i sgro btags*]" G 57. He divides into three: *rigs spyi, don spyi* and *tshogs spyi*. Cf. Dreyfus (1997: 107–109). Typology of spyi in Phya pa cf. Hugon (2008: 249–255).

Bod rgya tshad ma rig pa'i tshig mdzod gives the following definition: "Phenomenon which is solely imputed by conceptualization as an object that is not established on its own. These are non-compounded phenomena like space etc. that are there by way of excluding what is to be negated and must depend on arising of object universal [*yul rang ngos nas grub pa ma yin par rtog pas btags pa tsam gyi chos/ nam mkha' la sogs pa dgag bya bcad pa dang don spyi 'char ba la ltos dgos pa'i 'dus ma byas kyi chos rnams so/*];" *bod rgya tshad ma rig pa'i tshig mdzod* (1988: 200).

[36] Go rams pa defines object universal as follows: "imputation erroneously taking what is seen and conceptualization [of it] be one [*snang brtags gcig tu 'khrul ba'i sgro btags*]" G 57. *Bod rgya tshad ma rig pa'i tshig mdzod* gives the following definition: "Category of general appearance. An imputation establishing exclusively the conceptual appearance or it is an appearance in the mind similar to object. For example it is like a vase appearing in conceptualization [*spyi'i nang gses/ rtog pa'i snang ngo tsam du grub pa'i sgro brtags kyi cha'am don gyi cha 'dra blo la snang ba/ dper na/ rtog pa la snang ba'i bum pa lta bu'o/*]." *Bod rgya tshad ma rig pa'i tshig mdzod* (1988: 166).

[37] See p. 135 below.

[38] Cf. analysis of the status of *don spyi* in Stoltz (2006).

– and it is a crucial difference – between the two is the quality of providing the possibility of obtaining the particular. In this way the object universal – despite its mental nature – turns out to perform the function as every self-sufficiently existing particular and this function is making possible the obtainment of the particular.[39] It is not particular, as is clearly stated by Go rams pa, but one can say that to some extent it performs the function of particular. This twofold nature of the object universal is in fact the key to understanding the issue at stake in the polemics presented by Go rams pa in the most important sections of the last part of his commentary.

Western Research on Cognizable Object in *Tshad ma rigs gter*

Western research on the cognizable object in *Tshad ma rigs gter* is limited so far only to very few papers. First is a quite general review by Kapstein (2000), second is the advanced analysis of argumentation for nominalism at the beginning of *Tshad ma rigs gter* by Jonathan Stoltz (2006). Also Hugon (2008) analyzes the status of the particular in Sa skya Paṇḍita.

Kapstein discusses the first chapter of *Tshad ma rigs gter* in the context of what he calls "Tibetan Scholasticism." For him Sa skya Paṇḍita is a kind of Tibetan Aristotelian who tries to rationalize Buddhist religion with the help of Dharmakīrti's works treated as an organon. Sketching very shortly the problematics of *Tshad ma rigs gter* (translated by him rather unhappily as *Treasury of Epistemological Reason*),[40] Kapstein says that his "primary purpose here is to indicate something of the style of argumentation that Sa skya Paṇḍita employs in this context."[41] Unfortunatelly, the reader is not told what kind of "something" Kapstein has in mind, since he merely tries to recapitulate a few arguments of Tibetan philosopher with no analysis of particular style of argumentation or rhetoric. He starts with his translation of the initial fragment from the first chapter while choosing quite debatable terminology. Even though Kapstein declares that he concurs with Dreyfus,[42] who translated *don spyi* as "object universal," he renders it as "objective generality." At the same time he renders the corresponding term *sgra spyi* as "general term" neglecting the fact that they form a pair of well established

---

[39] Cf. the analysis of similar situation in Dharmakīrti in Dreyfus (1997: 74). It is thus clear that some difficult points discussed in Tibetan epistemology are in fact of Indian origin.

[40] Gererally Kapstein's use of philosophical terminology shows lack of real acquaintance with it. For example, *shes bya'i yul* (cognizable object or object of cognition) is translated by him strangely enough as "epistemological object."

[41] Kapstein (2000: 89).

[42] Cf. Kapstein (2000: 241, note 21).

complementary concepts rooted in Dignāga's distinction between *śabdasāmānya* and *arthasāmānya*[43] – and then, additionally, he misleads the reader by giving in brackets the term *ming spyi* while the original reads *sgra spyi*. The term *rang rig* is rendered as "self-presentation" instead of self-knowing or self-consciousness. The term *ldan pa ma yin pa 'du byed* is translated as "factors of being which are set apart." Giving *'du byed* as "factor of being" with regard to the factors which are neither associated with matter nor with mind is quite confusing. What kind of being is meant here? Absolute being or particular? Being as a process or as an entity?

Next Kapstein lists all the definitions of the objects based on Go rams pa's commentary. Unfortunately, here again he is not strict enough. For example, he gives the following definition of *'jug yul*: "That object which is the predominant [established] ground for an [epistemic] operation directed upon it by a corresponding subject."[44] Probably this was meant as a paraphrase of Go rams pa's definition (which is suggested by square brackets) but it is not accurate. The original text reads "the main one which is an object that became the basis for engagement making the subject and the thing compatible."[45] Thus Kapstein leaves out the most important part of the definition, namely compatibility between subject and object, which is a guarantee for the accuracy of cognition, and makes it correct, effective for presenting the object that can be acted upon.

When comparing the definitions he lists, I note that Kapstein elaborates on the synonymity of the term *yod nges* rendered as "certainly existent" and object understood as something that mind can be aware or conscious of. He is sure here that the reason for this synonymity is Buddhist idealism, claiming the same as Berkeley with his *esse est percipi*: "all that certainly exists and all that a mind can be aware of are mental acts."[46] This is of course not true because the theory of object in *pramāṇa* system is based on the Sautrāntika view, and here has nothing to do with idealism of Yogācāra implied by Kapstein. And this is exactly the type of flaw that the author Kapstein refers to, one that Dreyfus warns against.[47]

With this kind of introduction one can hardly expect a cogent analysis of the concept of object in Sa skya Paṇḍita, even if the author quotes fragments from Hume, Meinong, Husserl and Russell, which are only superficially associated with Sa skya Paṇḍita's work – thus showing a lack of deep comparative analysis that the author declared at the beginning of his text.

---

43 Cf. note 8 on page 91 below and Stewart (2010: 65–67).

44 Kapstein (2000: 90).

45 See p. 119 below.

46 Kapstein (2000: 91).

47 Cf. Dreyfus (1997: 76–79).

In the text "Sakya Pandita and the Status of Concepts" Jonathan Stoltz deals with nominalist arguments given in the first chapter of *Tshad ma rigs gter*. The author decides to translate *don spyi* as "concept," which is the translation faithful to the intention of Buddhist epistemology but has the disadvantage of obscuring the relation to Tibetan *sgra spyi* (preserved when we translate them respectively as "object universal" and "sound universal"). Nevertheless, as he himself says, Stoltz is aware that these are "less than perfect semantic matches,"[48] even though he still uses them, phrased in well-established European philosophical terminology for the sake of clarity of his argumentation.

Differentiating his approach from that of Dreyfus when discussing the status of universals in Tibetan philosophy, Stoltz claims that "the crux of the debate over concepts is really to be found within discussions of the philosophy of mind."[49] It is hard to disagree with this approach, since the very object – and concept was claimed to be an object – is defined as that what is cognizable by mind.

Stoltz begins his considerations with a very useful overview of the role of concepts in Tibetan tradition and sets up the general frame:

> While Sa-pan and his opponents do argue about whether universals exist in reality or in the mind, both parties agree that concepts are mentally constructed entities. Sa-pan's rejection of concepts is, therefore, a rejection of intersubjectively shareable mental entities. While his subsequent arguments in the *Treasure of Reasoning* against the existence of universals and materially composite entities center on the question of whether these general entities exist objectively or only as mental constructs, Sa-pan's arguments against concepts focus on the question of whether these purported mental entities could be epistemically evaluable objects at all.[50]

Then he goes on with precise analysis of two arguments presented by Sa skya Paṇḍita. The first one refers to the relation between valid/invalid conceptual cognition and valid/invalid object of it. The second one refers to intersubjectivity and possibility of the existence of private objects. It is quite remarkable that this kind of post-Wittgensteinian topic is addressed by thirteenth century Tibetan philosopher, and Stoltz's analysis shows Sa skya Paṇḍita to be really a modern philosopher.

Stoltz not only reconstructs the line of arguments of Sa skya Paṇḍita but also identifies their presuppositions and limitations. He intentionally introduces the

---

[48] Stoltz (2006: 579). Cf. also footnote 4. And also his proposal for translating *snang yul* is "phenomenal entity" and *zhen yul* – "implied entity," *gzung yul* – "cognitively held object."

[49] Stoltz (2006: 567).

[50] Stoltz (2006: 569).

notion of "robust existence"[51] as the existence of an epistemologically evaluable object. This term suggests the possibility of some vague existence of something that cannot be evaluated in this way – which is not the view of the author of *Tshad ma rigs gter*. Therefore, after Sa skya Paṇḍita this distinction can be questioned; but it still serves as a useful tool for explicating the problems raised at the beginning of the first chapter. It makes no sense to repeat here the author's whole analysis (which can be treated as a fair commentary to the polemical part of the chapter addressing the status of *don spyi*), so I jump straight to his conclusions:

> One thing that I do believe Sa-pan's arguments have done is to cast doubt on the views of his Tibetan philosophical predecessors by calling into question the necessity and worth of concepts. In his first argument, Sa-pan wishes to show that an acceptance of the existence of concepts would be incompatible with the entrenched view that conceptual thought is one-and-all unsound. Yet, even without proving this point, he does succeed in calling into doubt the perceived presumption on the part of his forerunners that all cognitions must have robustly existing phenomenal objects. The possibility that cognition – including mistaken/unsound cognition – can be explained without requiring that all cognitions refer to some robustly existing appearing entity suggests that one could apply Ockham's razor and shave away concepts without doing any harm to well-established views of mind and cognition. [...] With his second argument, Sa-pan has ventured to show that concepts, were they to exist, would only have the status of private, non-intersubjective, entities. As such, concepts would be epiphenomenal to most issues related to knowledge and cognition – and it is epistemology, not metaphysics itself, that Tibetan Buddhist thinkers hold to be most important. Thus, because concepts would play no epistemic role, they are theoretically dispensable posits.[52]

Stoltz rightly argues that in the end Sa skya Paṇḍita did not prove non-existence of concepts. Yet this was probably not his aim, since in this case he was – in the manner of good madhyamaka philosopher – just persuading the former tradition to abandon an incorrect view, hence his technique of *reductio ad absurdum* employed not only in the first chapter of *Tshad ma rigs gter*.

---

[51] Stoltz (2006: footnote 11).

[52] Stoltz (2006: 578).

Note on *Opening Verses*

Since the chapter on the cognizable object is the very beginning of *Tshad ma rigs gter* and, consequently, of commentary by Go rams pa, to make this beginning complete I also included the opening verses from both texts.

Sa skya Paṇḍita starts his opus magnum with characteristic *rgya gar skad du* (in the language of India) introducing Sanskrit title followed by *bod skad du* (in the language of Tibet) introducing Tibetan translation of it. *Tshad ma rigs gter* of course was written originally in Tibetan, however this kind of rhetorical gesture – used not only by Sa skya Paṇḍita – aims at presenting the text as faithful to Indian commentarial tradition of *bstan 'gyur* where every text translated into Tibetan starts in the same manner.

Sa skya Paṇḍita's treatise was written as a *śastra* so it has to have the characteristic fourfold structure: expression of worship (*mchod brjod*) by way of paying homage, promise or pledge of composing the text (*rtsom par bca'*), the body of the text (*dngos kyi don*) and dedication (*bsngo ba*). The opening verses include the first two parts and are followed by short outline of the whole text.

The homage is paid to *Mañjuśrī*, bodhisattva dwelling on the tenth *bhūmi* who is called *gzhon nur gyur pa* (Skr. *kumārabhūta*) – the one who became young. This epithet stresses the fact that *Mañjuśrī* has the body of a sixteen--year-old man, which symbolizes his state of perfection, since the age of sixteen is considered the moment when the powers and capacities of the body are at their peak. Paying homage at the beginning of Buddhist text has several purposes. First one is erasing the pride of the author of the text, which is considered the main hindrance in gathering knowledge. Thus in this way the author opens up to the source of Buddhist wisdom embodied by *Mañjuśrī*. The reader should of course follow the example of the author and pay homage himself and both of them should do it traditionally with the so called three gates meaning body (bowing down physically), speech (pronouncing the mantra of *Mañjuśrī*) and mind (focusing on the imagined form of *Mañjuśrī*). In this way all hindrances to presenting and absorbing dharma are erased or swept away, as Tibetans often explain that the formula *phyag 'tshal* refers not only to folding hands (*phyag*) in the gesture of reverence but also to sweeping away (*phyags*) obstacles and purifying a mind.

In Buddhist tradition choosing *Mañjuśrī* as an object of homage shows also the basket the text belongs to. The homage paid to Buddha himself opens the texts belonging to *Vinaya* basket, the homage to Buddha and Bodhisattvas – *Sūtra* basket, and the homage to *Mañjuśrī* – the basket of *Abhidharma*. Thus *Tshad ma rigs gter* belongs of course to *abhīdharma*, since Buddhist epistemology can be considered the crown of *abhīdharma* teachings.

After praising *Mañjuśrī*, Sa skya Paṇḍita continues by praising his lama in terms of the so called three qualities [*yon tan*] – wisdom, kindness and power [*mkhyen brtse nus gsum*] – and thus he can be perceived as inseparable from Bodhisattva of Wisdom himself.

Next Sa skya Paṇḍita invokes the two among the so called six ornaments beautifying *Jambudvīpa* (*'dzam gling mdzes pa'i rgyan drug*),[53] namely Nāgārjuna and Dharmakīrti, in order to seal his understanding of emptiness and epistemology. Relying on this threefold authority Sa skya Paṇḍita goes on by pointing out lack of understanding of Dharmakīrti's philosophy in Tibet, presenting himself as the one who is to reintroduce it in a way that is free of previous faults and misunderstandings.

It the last four verses of the opening lines Sa skya Paṇḍita gives his promise to compose his text that will elucidate Dharmakīrtian epistemology in the best way possible guaranteed with his impartial attitude full of compassion and genuine knowledge.

Opening lines of Go rams pa's commentary are shorter and composed of two stanzas. The first one is very elaborate and poetic invocation to body, speech and mind of *Mañjuśrī*, who is not called by his name. The second stanza is much more formal reference to the tradition of Dignāga and Dharmakīrti, promising faultless explanation to fortunate readers.

Translation and edition

What follows is annotated translation and edition of the first chapter of *Tshad ma rigs gter* by Sa skya Paṇḍita and the corresponding first chapter of Go rams pa's commentary *Tshad ma rigs pa'i gter gyi don gsal bar byed pa*. These two texts together are probably the best point of departure for studies on the notion of cognizable object in Sa skya Paṇḍita.

In the first chapter of *Tshad ma rigs gter* on the cognizable object Sa skya Paṇḍita gives no definition of the technical terms that he uses throughout the text. From the very beginning the reader finds himself in the very center of an intensely heated philosophical debate, which presupposes not only the knowledge of basic terminology but also the whole philosophical background out of which the problems discussed are picked up. Thus the tasks of the commentarial tradition of the *Tshad ma rigs gter* include clarifying terminology within the conceptual system used in this treatise and contextualizing the problems discussed, with possible solutions offered by different traditions of Tibetan epistemology.

[53] The remaining four are of course: Asaṅga, Vasubandhu, Dignāga, Āryadeva.

This clear division of commentarial work is probably the reason why Go rams pa (*go rams pa bsod nams seng ge*, 1429–1489) wrote two commentaries to the *Tshad ma rigs gter*, namely *sDe bdun mdo dang bcas pa'i dgongs pa phin ci ma log par 'grel ba tshad ma rigs pa'i gter gyi don gsal bar byed pa* (*The Faultless Commentary on the Intention of Seven Treatises and the Sutra Elucidating the Meaning of* [Sa skya Paṇḍita's] Treasury of Epistemology) and *Tshad ma rigs gter gyi dka' gnas rnam par bshad pa sde bdun rab gsal* (*The Complete Explanation of Difficult Points in* Treasury of Epistemology *that is a Perfect Elucidation of Seven Treatises*). The first one is very encyclopedic and can be treated as an introduction to the second,[54] since the first one – as the title announces – is just an explanation of general intention of the treatise and mainly aims at clarifying terminology used in the *Tshad ma rigs gter*. The second one, much more extensive, concentrates on particular epistemological problems and, as the title says, "difficult points" debated in Tibetan epistemology. It is much more elaborate and goes much deeper into the issues discussed in the text of Sa skya Paṇḍita, which now can be clearly restated in the light of the first commentary and then solved. The first commentary can also be treated as a kind of shortcut to Sa skya Paṇḍita's philosophy, providing an especially clear map of the system – following Go rams pa's famous, unique ability to present complicated matters in a very accessible way.

Thus the whole conceptual and terminological frame together with basic definitions of the first chapter of *Tshad ma rigs gter* can be found in Go rams pa's commentary. It is probably true that nobody who studies Sa skya Paṇḍita's *Tshad ma rigs gter* can avoid referring to Go rams pa's commentaries on this work, as he or she searches for the answers to the numerous questions that appear during the lecture. Sa skya Paṇḍita usually takes for granted that the reader knows the basic definitions and the necessary context. However, what might be obvious to the philosophical audience in the thirteen century in Tibet is definitely not obvious to a modern reader in the West. Even though Sa skya Paṇḍita's auto-commentary clarifies a lot of issues from the root text, its reading, said without any exaggeration, must be accompanied or maybe even preceded by a study of some more encyclopedic commentary like Go rams pa's *sDe bdun mdo dang bcas pa'i dgongs pa phin ci ma log par 'grel ba tshad ma rigs pa'i gter gyi don gsal bar byed pa*. That commentary provides a clear conceptual frame for discussing the *Tshad ma rigs gter* and also for solving intensely debated problems. Go rams pa calls it "elucidation of the meaning [*don gsal bar byed pa*]," and this, indeed, is what he tries to do by giving a neat map of the terminology that

[54] Go rams pa has the very same approach in the case of his two commentaries to *Pramāṇavārttika*. Cf. van der Kuijp (1983: 122).

can serve as a general framework for reading Sa skya Paṇḍita's work. Written in an accessible style, supplying basic definitions and sketching the main ideas and contexts, it is particularly helpful as both a prolegomenon and companion to the *Tshad ma rigs gter*. On top of that, Go rams pa is considered the most faithful and orthodox commentator of Sa skya Paṇḍita[55] because he does not depart from the original meaning and intention of the *Tshad ma rigs gter*.[56] That is why, out of so many commentaries to *Tshad ma rigs gter*, both within Sa skya tradition and others,[57] *Don gsal bar byed pa* by Go rams pa is probably one of the most natural starting points for our reception of this fundamental treatise of Tibetan epistemology. Acknowledged conformity of Go rams pa's interpretation with the *Tshad ma rigs gter* also makes his text a very good starting point for investigating interpretational differences within Sa skya lineage itself and gives a clear point of reference for comparative studies of *s*Ge lugs and rNying ma interpretations of the *Tshad ma rigs gter*[58] as well.

Both editions presented in this volume are diplomatic and modest (I didn't engage in a full-fledged critical edition including all textual witnesses). The system used for the transcription of the Tibetan texts is Wylie. The structure of the editions follows *sa bcad*. The number of *sa bcad* with the title of *sa bcad* is added in square brackets []. The words inserted by translator are also in square brackets.

The reference to folio numbers of the original text is given in pointed brackets <>. The division between objection (indicated with *zhe na*) and the answer of the author is marked in square brackets with the name of the author giving the answer.

In case of abbreviations like *mtshid* for *mtshan nyid* it is preserved in the main text and the extended form is indicated in the footnote if it was used in later edition. Root verses (*rtsa ba*) are written in italics and with indentation on both

---

55 The lineage of transmission from Sa skya Paṇḍita to Go rams pa, cf. van der Kuijp (1983: 118). His contemporary *Śākya mchog ldan* (*gser mdog pan chen śākya mchog ldan*, 1428–1509) was no less a perceptive commentator of *Tshad ma rigs gter* but definitely a less orthodox thinker adhering also to the view of other-emptiness [*gzhan stong*] fought against by Go rams pa (more about his refusal of this view cf. J.I. Cabezón, D. Lobsang (2006: 97–144).

56 Cf. Dreyfus (1997: 27).

57 Cf. short description of all commentaries to *Tshad ma rigs gter* in Hugon (2008: 124–127).

58 In particular, the most interesting commentaries are that of Klo bo mkhan chen bsod nam lhun grub, ShAkya mchog ldan, rGyal tshab dar ma rin chen, *Tshad ma rigs pa'i gter gyi dka' gnas* by Go rams pa and the latest commentary by 'Jam mgon 'ju mi pham rnam rgyal rgya mtsho. There is no commentary to the *Tshad ma rigs gter* written in the bka' brgyud tradition, but very interesting polemics with Sa skya Paṇḍita can be found in the *Tshad ma rigs gzhung rgya mtsho* (*The Ocean of Epistemological Treatises*) by 7th Karma pa Chos grags rgya mtsho (1454–1506). Cf. Przybyslawski (2016: 394–395).

sides and with verse number in slash brackets //. Quotations are written with an indentation on both sides as well but are not in italics.

In the case of *Tshad ma rigs pa'i gter* the oldest Mongol xylograph version (*hor par ma*) – which "perhaps, also constitutes the earliest Tibetan blockprint as such"[59] – is reproduced here and variant readings given in footnotes follow the editions:

T1 – *Tshad ma rigs pa'i gter gyi rtsa ba dang 'grel*. Varanasi, Sarnath: Central Institute of Higher Tibetan Studies (Sakya Students' Union), 48–68.

T2 – *Tshad ma rigs pa'i gter gyi rang 'brel*, in: *dpal ldan sa skya pa'i bka' bum* (reproduced from the 1736 Derge Edition), New Delhi: Sakya Center 1993, vol. 11 (*da*), 52–71.

In the case of Go rams pa's commentary the original reproduced is that of collected works of Go rams pa:

Kun-mkhyen go-rams-pa bsod-nams-seṅge'i gsuṅ 'bum, Dehra-Dun: Sakya College 1996, vol. 2, 387–400.

The text was compared with the two latest editions of Go rams pa's commentary:

K1 – *Dpal sa skya pa'i tshad ma rig pa'i gzhung gces bsdus*, New Delhi: Institute of Tibetan Classics 2006 (*bod kyi gtsug lag gces bdus*, vol. 20), 40–49.

K2 – *Tshad ma rigs gter rtsa ba dang 'grel pa bzhugs*, Sichuan: People's Press 2008, 68–79.

59 Van der Kuijp (1993a: 280).

EDITION AND TRANSLATION OF THE FIRST CHAPTER OF *TSHAD MA RIGS GTER*

rgya gar skad du| pra mA Na yug ta ni d+hi| bod skad du tshad ma rigs pa'i gter||
'phags pa 'jam dpal gzhon nur gyur pa la gus pas phyag 'tshal lo||

shes bya thams cad gzigs pa'i spyan yangs pa||
'gro kun dge legs sgrub pa'i thugs je can||
bsam yas phrin las mdzad pa'i stobs mnga ba||
'jam mgon bla ma'i zhabs la mgos phyag 'tshal||
blo gros spyi gtsug yon tan nor bu'i rgyan gyis spras||
bden gnyis ro 'dzin stong nyid phud sgra'i sgra sgrogs shing||
mkhyen brtse'i lta zer phas rgol skye bas mi bzod pa||
blo gsal rgya mtsho'i rgyan gyur dpal ldan klu dbang rgyal||
gangs ri'i khrod 'dir mkhas pa'i rgyu skar bye ba brgyas||
dpal ldan grags pa'i gsung rab pad+mo rab phye mod||
gang blo'i nyi 'od snang bas ma khyab de srid du||
gzhung lugs dgongs don ge sar snying po gsal ma nus||
chos kyi grags pa'i bzhed gzhung ji lta bar||
blo gros gsal ba'i mig gis legs mthong nas||
shes ldan gzu bor gnas pa don gnyer ba||
gzhan la brtse ba'i bdam pas 'di bshad do||

yang dag pa'i shes pa dag la rigs pa smra bar khas 'che ba rnams kyang log par rtog pa du ma mthong bas de sun dbyang ba dang yang dag pa'i don gtan la dbab pa'i phyir 'di brtsam mo||

de la gnyis te shes bya spyi ldog nas gtan la dbab pa dang| shes byed tshad ma'i rang bzhin nges par bya ba'o| |dang po la gsum ste| shes bya'i yul| shes byed kyi blo| blo des yul rtogs pa'i tshul lo||

Opening verses of *Tshad ma rigs gter*

In the language of India: *Pramāṇayuktanidhi*
In the language of Tibet: *Tshad ma rigs pa'i gter* [*Treasury of Epistemology*]

Homage with reverence to *Ārya Mañjuśrī kumārabhūta*!
You with far reaching eyes that see all that is cognizable
Who have compassion accomplishing excellence among all samsaric beings,
Possessing the power to perform inconceivable [enlightened] activity,[1]
I pay homage with my head at the foot of the Lama,[2] who is Gentle Protector.[3]
Intelligence adorns the crown on [your] head with the jewel ornament of qualities,
With the tongue tasting two truths, you proclaim the hiss of emptiness.[4]
The rays of your view of wisdom and compassion is unbearable for opponents.
You became the ornament of the ocean of clear intelligence and mighty Lord of Nāgās [Nāgārjuna] who is victorious.
Here in The Land of Snowy Mountains milliard stars of sages
Make the lotus of the teachings of the glorious [Dharma-]Kīrti open.[5]
While the radiance of the sun-rays of somebody's intelligence did not flare up,
The pistil-like core of the meaning intended in the scriptures could not be clarified.[6]
With the eye of clear intelligence perfectly perceiving
The view and treatises of Dharmakīrti as they are,
And then with the mind endowed with the knowledge, aspiring to be impartial, and loving others, I explained them.

Among the proponents of theories of true cognitions there are some who fail to notice wrong conceptions. So this [text] was composed in order to disprove them and to proclaim the real meaning.
Here [in this text] are the two parts: establishing general field of knowledge and ascertaining the essence of valid cognition that performs the act of knowledge.[7]
In the first part there are three subparts: cognizable object, cognizing mind and the way this mind apprehends the object.[8]

Notes

[1] These three lines describe the lama in terms of three qualities: wisdom, kindness and power, cf. Introduction.

[2] Sa skya Paṇḍita's lama is not named in his text while *'jam mgon bla ma* is only a honorific epithet (explained in the next footnote). Blo bo mkhan chen bsod nams lhun grub does not mention any name in his commentary; Shākya mchog ldan says only that his root lama [rtsa ba'i bla ma] is meant here. However, g.Yag ston sangs rgyas dpal in his commentary identifies him as rje btsun grags pa rgyal mtshan (1147–1216) – the uncle of Sa skya Paṇḍita. For more information on him, cf. van der Kuijp (1983: 98–99).

[3] The epithet explained by the above mentioned g.yag ston sangs rgyas dpal signifies the inseparability of the lama and Mañjuśrī, who is called Gentle Protector.

[4] A metaphor expressing the fact that Buddhist teachings on emptiness proclaimed by Nāgārjuna as Snake-Nāgā Conqueror are frightening for non-Buddhist philosophers.

[5] Invoking Nāgārjuna and Dharmakīrti together in *pramāṇa* context is characteristic of the approach introduced by Rngog Blo ldan shes rab who combined their philosophies. Cf. Jackson (1987: 166–168).

[6] Cf. comment on these verses in Hugon (2012: 28). Her translation is however slightly different: "In this snowy mountain range, thanks to the hundred millions of constellations of scholars the lotus of the teachings of the Glorious [Dharma-]kīrti blossoms. Nevertheless, insofar as these [scholars] are not pervaded by the sunrays of intelligence, they are unable to throw light on the heart of its pistil, the intended meaning of the texts." Most probably, Hugon takes the phrase "gang blo'i nyi 'od snang bas ma khyab" as "gang la blo'i nyi 'od snang bas ma khyab." After consulting a native speaker I take it as "gang gi blo'i nyi 'od snang bas ma khyab." This line is in fact the introduction of Sa skya Paṇḍita himself as the one who is to clarify Buddhist epistemology, so the intention behind the phrase "somebody's intelligence" is the mind of the author of *Tshad ma rigs gter*. This reading is also confirmed by g.Yag ston sangs rgyas dpal in his commentary where this this passage is explained as follows: "bdag gi blo gros nyi ma'i 'od lta bu'i snang bas ma khyab kyi". g.Yag ston sangs rgyas dpal (2007: 422).

[7] *Tshad ma rigs gter* is generally divided into two parts. The first part – "establishing general field of knowledge" – includes the chapters 1–7, namely: 1) Analysis of object [*yul brtag pa*], 2) Analysis of mind [*blo brtag pa*], 3) Analysis of the universal and the particular [*spyi dang bye brag brtag pa*], 4) Analysis of proof and exclusion [*sgrub pa dang gzhan sel brtag pa*], 5) Analysis

of signified and signifier [*brjod bya dang rjod byed*], 6) Analysis of relation [*'brel ba brtag pa*], 7) Analysis of contradiction [*'gal ba brtag pa*].

The second part – "Ascertaining the essence of valid cognition that performs the act of knowledge" – includes the chapters 8–11, namely: 8) Analysis of defining characteristics [*mtshan nyid brtag pa*], 9) Analysis of direct perception [*mngon sum brtag pa*], 10) Analysis of inference for the sake of oneself [*rang don rjes dpag brtag pa*], 11) Analysis of inference for the sake of others [*gzhan don rjes dpag brtag pa*]. More on the structure of *Tshad ma rigs gter* cf. Hugon (2008: 109–111).

[8] First two subparts are first and second chapter of *Tshad ma rigs gter* accordingly. The third subpart includes chapters 3–7.

sa bcad

1. mtshan nyid

2. dbye ba
   2.1. gzhan gyi lugs dgag pa
      2.1.1. khas blangs brjod pa
      2.1.2. dgag pa
         2.1.2.1. blo ma 'khrul bar thal ba
         2.1.2.2. yul snang rung du thal ba
   2.2. rang gi 'dod pa brjod pa
   2.3. rtsod pa spang pa
      2.3.1. 'khrul shes yul med la rtsod pa spang pa
         2.3.1.1. gzhal bya gnyis su gsungs pa dang 'gal ba spang pa
         2.3.1.2. don spyi dang med pa gsal ba yul du mtshungs pa'i rtsod pa spang pa
         2.3.1.3. myong ba dang 'gal ba spang pa
         2.3.1.4. dgag pa tshad mas mi rtogs par thal ba spang ba
      2.3.2. gzung yul rang mtshan la rtsod pa spang ba
         2.3.2.1. rtsod pa dgod pa
         2.3.2.2. lan
            2.3.2.2.1. grub mtha'i rnam gzhag spyir dpyad pa
            2.3.2.2.2. gzhan gyis brtags pa dgag pa
            2.3.2.2.3. bde bar gshegs pa'i lugs bsgrub pa
               2.3.2.2.3.1. dgongs pa ngos gzung pa
               2.3.2.2.3.2. slob dpon gyis ji ltar gtan la phab pa'i tshul
                  2.3.2.2.3.2.1. don rig
                     2.3.2.2.3.2.1.1. gzhan lugs dgag pa
                        2.3.2.2.3.2.1.1.1. bye brag du smra ba'i lugs dgag pa
                        2.3.2.2.3.2.1.1.2. bod kyi lugs dgag pa

Outline of *Tshad ma rigs gter* I

1. Definition

2. Division
  2.1. Refutation of other systems
    2.1.1. Presentation of the position to be refuted
    2.1.2. Refutation
      2.1.2.1. (Paradoxical) consequence of non-erroneous mind
      2.1.2.2. (Paradoxical) consequence that object can appear to others
  2.2. Presentation of our own position
  2.3. Rebuttal of objections
    2.3.1. Rebuttal of the objection to the nonexistent object of erroneous cognition
      2.3.1.1. Rebuttal of the contradiction with the statement that there are two perceptibles
      2.3.1.2. Rebuttal of the objection that object universal and nonexistent clearly (appearing) are similar objects
      2.3.1.3. Rebuttal of what contradicts the experience
      2.3.1.4. The rebuttal of the (paradoxical) conclusion of the negation being not realized by valid cognition
    2.3.2. Rebuttal of the objection to the apprehended object as a particular
      2.3.2.1. Determining the objection
      2.3.2.2. Answer
        2.3.2.2.1. Analysis of the general presentation of tenet system
        2.3.2.2.2. Refutation of others' theories
        2.3.2.2.3. Establishing the system of Sugata
          2.3.2.2.3.1. Identifying the intent
          2.3.2.2.3.2. The way the ācārya settled the question
            2.3.2.2.3.2.1. Knowledge of entity
              2.3.2.2.3.2.1.1. Refutation of other systems
                2.3.2.2.3.2.1.1.1. Refutation of the Vaibhāṣika system
                2.3.2.2.3.2.1.1.2. Refutation of Tibetan systems

2.3.2.2.3.2.1.2. rang lugs rjod pa
2.3.2.2.3.2.1.3. rtsod pa spang pa
2.3.2.2.3.2.2. rnam rig
2.3.2.2.3.2.2.1. gzhan gyis brtags pa dgag pa
2.3.2.2.3.2.2.1.1. phyi rol gyi don grub pa dgag pa
2.3.2.2.3.2.2.1.2. 'jig rten grags pa la brten pa dgag pa
2.3.2.2.3.2.2.2. rnam par rig pa bsgrub pa
2.3.2.2.3.2.2.2.1. shes pa'i mtshan nyid
2.3.2.2.3.2.2.2.2. lhan gcig dmigs nges kyis 'grub pa
2.3.2.2.3.2.2.2.2.1. rtags dgod pa
2.3.2.2.3.2.2.2.2.2. rtags de'i tshul bsgrub pa
2.3.2.2.3.2.2.2.2.3. rtsod pa spang pa
2.3.2.2.3.2.2.2.2.3.1. btsun pa dge bsrungs la stsogs pa'i rtsod pa spang ba
2.3.2.2.3.2.2.2.2.3.2. rtags 'di 'gal bas pang ba
2.3.2.2.3.2.2.2.2.3.3. gtan tshigs 'di ma nges pa spang ba
2.3.2.2.3.2.2.3. rnam rig la rtsod pa spang ba
2.3.2.2.3.2.2.3.1. rig pa'i rtags ma grub pa spang ba
2.3.2.2.3.2.2.3.2. rdul phran dang mtshungs pa spang ba
2.3.2.2.3.2.2.3.3. rnam pa yong med la brtags na mi 'thad pa spang pa

2.3.2.2.3.2.1.2. Presentation of our system
2.3.2.2.3.2.1.3. Rebuttal of objections
2.3.2.2.3.2.2. Knowledge through the aspect
2.3.2.2.3.2.2.1. Refutation of investigation made by others
2.3.2.2.3.2.2.1.1. Refutation of the outer entity
2.3.2.2.3.2.2.1.2. Refutation of relying on worldly opinions
2.3.2.2.3.2.2.2. Establishment of knowledge through the aspect
2.3.2.2.3.2.2.2.1. Definition of consciousness
2.3.2.2.3.2.2.2.2. Establishing by way of concurrent perception
2.3.2.2.3.2.2.2.2.1. Necessity of the reason
2.3.2.2.3.2.2.2.2.2. Establishment of the modes of this reason
2.3.2.2.3.2.2.2.2.3. Rebuttal of the objections
2.3.2.2.3.2.2.2.2.3.1. Rebuttal of the objection of bTsun pa dGe bSrung and others
2.3.2.2.3.2.2.2.2.3.2. Rebuttal of contradiction to this reasoning
2.3.2.2.3.2.2.2.2.3.3. Rebuttal of claim that this argumentation is not ascertained
2.3.2.2.3.2.2.3. Rebuttal of objections concerning knowledge through the aspect
2.3.2.2.3.2.2.3.1. Rebuttal of [statement that] reasoning proving knowledge is not established
2.3.2.2.3.2.2.3.2. Rebuttal of the objection that (act knowledge) is similar to the atom
2.3.2.2.3.2.2.3.3. Rebuttal (of argumentation that) if aspects are examined whether they exist or not, they are not acceptable

[yul brtag pa]

<2a> dang po la gnyis las|

[1. mtshan nyid]
mtshan nyid ni|

> *yul gyi mtshan nyid blos rig bya*|| /1a/

[2. dbye ba]
gnyis pa dbye ba la gsum gyi

[2.1. gzhan gyi lugs dgag pa]
dang po gzhan gyi lugs dgag pa la[1] gnyis las|

[2.1.1. khas blangs brjod pa]
dang po khas blangs[2] brjod na|

> *don spyi dang ni med snang gnyis*|
> *yul yin zhe na*| /1bc/

bod rnams rtog pa 'khrul pa'i yul don spyi dang| rtog med 'khrul pa'i yul med pa gsal ba gnyis med na 'khrul pa gzhi med du 'gyur bas snang yul gnyis yong la| de 'ang 'khrul shes gnyis 'dzin pa'i rang rig mngon sum gyi shugs[3] la grub bo zhes zer ba dang| nyan thos sde pa mang pos bkur ba la sogs pa kha cig[4] sgra spyi dang don spyi gnyis ming dang mtshan ma'i rnam pa can gzugs dang sems dang sems las byung pa[5] dang mi ldan pas ldan pa ma yin pa'i 'du byed rdzas su grub par

---

[1] *la* omitted in T2.
[2] T1, T2: blang
[3] T1, T2: rang rig gi shugs
[4] *kha cig* omitted in T2.
[5] T1, T2: ba

[Object Analysis]

The first [chapter of *Tshad ma rigs gter*] has two [parts].

[1. Definition]
[The first one is] the following definition:

Definition of the object: that which is knowable by mind. /1a/

[2. Division]
In the second [part], the first among the three [parts] is

[2.1. Refutation of other systems]
Refutation of other systems in two parts as follows

[2.1.1. Presentation of the position to be refuted]
The first part is a presentation of the position:

Both object universal[1] *and nonexistent appearing*[2] *are objects, they say...* /1bc/

Tibetans say[3] "if both conceptual erroneous object which is an object universal and nonconceptual erroneous object which is a nonexistent clearly [appearing] do not exist, then there would be no basis of error, therefore [these] two appearing objects[4] do exist.[5] Moreover, there are two erroneous cognitions established with the power of self-knowing perception that apprehends [them]."[6] The Śrāvaka [schools], such as the Sāṃmitīya,[7] and so forth, assert that neither sound universal[8] nor object universal is associated either with [physical] form or with mind, or with mental acts,[9] that have the aspects of name and characteristics, so that is why [these] nonassociated factors[10] are established as substance.[11]

'dod la| med pa gsal ba rmi lam gyi yul yang don gyi mtshan ma mi ldan pa'i 'du byed ces bya ba rdzas su grub pa de las rmi lam gyi shes pa skye bar 'dod do||

[2.1.2. dgag pa]
gnyis pa de dgag pa la gnyis las|

[2.1.2.1. blo ma 'khrul bar thal ba]
dang po blo ma 'khrul bar thal ba ni|

de 'dzin gyi||
shes pa gnyis po 'khrul par 'gal|| /1cd/

don spyi dang skra shad la stsogs[6] pa yul yin na de dag 'dzin[7] pa'i rtog pa dang mig shes gnyis ma 'khrul bar 'gyur te| yul yod pa'i phyir bum 'dzin gyi mig shes bzhin no|| gal te khyab pa mi 'grub ste|

yul yod na 'ang[8] thag ba la||
sbrul[9] 'dzin bzhin du 'khrul ce[10] na|| /2ab/

yul yod kyang thag pa la sbrul du 'dzin pa dang nya phyis la dngul du 'dzin pa bzhino ce[11] na|

khrar 'dzin yul yod phyir ma 'khrul||
yul med pas na sbrul 'dzin 'khrul|| /2cd/

thag pa'i khra bo kha dog gi rdul dngos <2b> po la grub pa'i phyir khra bor snang pa'i[12] mig shes skabs der yang ma 'khrul la| sbrul don la ma grub pa rtog pas sgro btags pa[13] yin pas yul med pa bzang ba'i phyir rtog pa 'khrul pa yin no||

---

[6] T1, T2: sogs
[7] T1, T2: de 'dzin
[8] T1, T2: yang
[9] T1, T2: sprul
[10] T2: zhe
[11] T1, T2: bzhin no zhe
[12] T1, T2: ba'i
[13] *pa* omitted in T2.

Object in the dream which is nonexistent clearly appearing, and also the so-called nonassociated factors of the characteristics of an entity are established as substance, and because of that they assert that cognition of a dream is produced.

[2.1.2. Refutation]

The second part is a refutation in two parts.

[2.1.2.1. (Paradoxical) consequence of non-erroneous mind]

The first one is [a paradoxical] consequence of non-erroneous mind:[12]

> *Both cognitions that apprehend them* [object universal and nonexistent clearly appearing] *contradict* [their own] *erroneous* [character].[13] /1cd/

If object universal and strand of hair[14], etc., were objects, then both conceptualization and eye consciousness that apprehends them would not be erroneous because of having [that] objects; it would be similar to an eye consciousness apprehending a vase. This [however] does not apply to all cases;

> *If they have objects, they would be erroneous as in the case of apprehending a rope as a snake,*[15] *they say...* /2ab/

They have objects but they would be like apprehending a rope as a snake and mother-of-pearl as silver, the say [so Sa skya Paṇḍita answers:]

> *Apprehending of glistening has an object, and that is why it is not erroneous. Apprehending of the snake is erroneous because it does not have an object.* /2cd/

The glistening of the rope is established on [the basis of] the thing [containing] particles of color, and that is why at the moment the eye consciousness perceives the color it is also not erroneous. Since conceptualization is not established [on the basis of] the snake as entity, it is imputation. That is why because of apprehending non-existent object, conceptualization is erroneous.

[2.1.2.2. yul snang rung du thal ba]
gnyis pa yul snang rung du thal ba ni|

snang yul gnyis po shes pa las||
tha dad yin na yul rung par[14]*||*
gnas pa'i gang zag gzhan gyis kyang||
mthong 'gyur bum pa la stsogs[15] *bzhin||* /3/

don spyi dang med pa gsal ba gnyis shes pa las tha dad pa'i yul zhig yin na| yul rnam pa ni rigs| yid nye bar gtad pa ni yod| 'khrul pa'i rgyu mtshan ni med pas yul snang rung gcig na gnas pa'i gang zag gzhan gyis kyang mthong bar 'gyur te| yul snang rung du khyad par med pa'i phyir bum pa thams cad kyis mthong pa[16] bzhin no|| de skad du 'ang rnam 'grel las|

rnam pa de ni tha dad na||
gzhan gyis de bzhin rtogs[17] *par 'gyur*[*] *zhes gsungs pa ltar ro||*

don nyid yin yang[18] *lus kyi nang||*
mi mthong bzhin du 'khrul snang gnyis||
bdag la rtag tu 'brel pa'i phyir||
gzhan gyis rtogs pa med ce na|| /4/

don spyi dang med pa gsal ba gnyis po yul du grub kyang rang gi lus kyi nang na gnas pa'i glo snying don[19] yin yang mi mthong pa[20] ltar gzhan gyis mi mthong ste| bdag gi blo dang 'brel pa'i phyir ro zhe na|

nang gi lus ni yul rung min||
des na rang gis kyang mi mthong|| /5ab/

---

[*] PV III 376ab: vyatiriktaṃ tam ākāraṃ pratīyād aparas tathā |
[14] T1, T2: bar
[15] T1, T2: sogs
[16] T2: ba
[17] T1, T2: gzhan gyis kyang ni rtogs
[18] T1, T2: kyang
[19] T1, T2: gnas pa don
[20] T1, T2: ba

[2.1.2.2. (Paradoxical) consequence that object can appear to others]

The second part [of the refutation], is the [paradoxical] consequence that object can appear [to other people].[16]

> *If both appearing objects are different from cognition, then the second person staying next to* [that kind of] *possible object will see it as well, as in the case of a vase, etc. /3/*

If both object universal and nonexistent clearly [appearing] are an object different from cognition, then since

- the aspects of the object are gross [apparent],
- there is the focusing of the mind [on it],
- there is no reason for being erroneous,

the second person staying next to that possible appearing object will see it as well. This is because there is no difference in the object that can appear, just like when everybody can see the vase. Thus it is said also in *Pramāṇavārttika*:

> if these aspects [of the object and cognition] are different, the other one will also realize [that object].[17]

> *It is precisely the meaning, but in the same way that* [we] *do not see entrails, the other* [person] *does not realize them because both erroneous appearances are always related to myself, they say. /4/*

Even though both object universal and nonexistent [appearing] clearly are established as objects, the second [person] does not see them as one doesn't see entrails, even though they are an entity. And this is because they are related to my own mind, they say [so Sa skya Paṇḍita answers:]

> *Entrails cannot be an object, because even I myself do not see them. /5ab/*

nang gi lus mi mthong ba dper mi rung ste| de ni yul rung ba ma yin pa'i phyir rang nyid kyis kyang mi mthong la| rung pa[21] na gnas na mthong par[22] 'gyur ro||

rang dang rtag tu 'brel pas[23] na||
gnyis po 'ang yul rung min ce[24] na|| /5cd/

gal te don spyi dang skra shad gnyis kyang gzhan gyi snang du rung pa'i[25] yul ma yin gyi rang gi blo dang dus rgyun du 'brel bas[26] so snyam na|

rang blo kho na dang 'brel phyir||
rjod[27] kyang gzhan gyis rtogs mi 'gyur|| /6ab/

rang rang gi blo kho na dang 'brel na rang rig pa bzhin du gzhan la bstan kyang go bar mi 'gyur ro|| de 'ang rnam 'grel las|

bdag la rtag tu 'brel yin na||
rjod[28] kyang rtogs par mi <3a> 'gyur ro[*] zhes gsungs pa ltar ro||

rang rang blo dang 'brel pa'i phyir||
rjod[29] pas de nyid rtogs ce[30] na|| /6cd/

gang zag rang rang gi blo dang 'brel ba'i[31] phyir rang gi blo'i yul de rjod[32] pas rang rang gi yul de go ba mi 'gal lo ce[33] na|

gang zag gnyis kyi brjod bya'i don||
so so yin phyir sbyor mi nus|| /7ab/

---

[*] PV III 376cd: nityam ātmani sambandhe pratīyāt kathitaṃ ca na ||
[21] T1, T2: ba
[22] T1, T2: bar
[23] T1, T2: bas
[24] T1, T2: zhe
[25] T1, T2: ba'i
[26] T1, T2: pas
[27] T1, T2: brjod
[28] T1, T2: brjod
[29] T1, T2: brjod
[30] T1, T2: she
[31] T1, T2: pa'i
[32] T1, T2: brjod
[33] T1, T2: zhe

Not seeing my entrails cannot be an example. Since they cannot be an object, even I myself do not see them. If they can be an object, being there one would see them.

> *Because they are always related to oneself, both also cannot be an object* [for others], *they say...* /5cd/

If one wonders: "an object universal and a strand of hair cannot be objects appearing to the other, but they are constantly related to my own mind, so [etc.]," then

> *Since they are related to my mind only, even though* [one can] *explain them, the other will not realize.* /6ab/

If they are related only to my own mind, even though I describe it to the other [person] as I know it, it will not be understood.[18] With regard to that, it is also similarly said in *Pramāṇavārttika*:

> Since it is constantly related to myself, then even though it is explained it will not be realized.[19]

> *Since one is related to one's own mind, then because of explaining, exactly this will be understood, they say...* /6cd/

Since a person is related to his or her own mind, then because of explaining that object of one's own mind, one's own object will be understood and there is no contradiction in it, they say [so Sa skya Paṇḍita answers:]

> *The entity that is explained to both persons is individual, so connection is impossible.*[20] /7ab/

gang zag rang rang gi blo dang 'brel pa rkyang pa de rjod[34] pas rang rang gi blo dang 'brel pa de go ba'i phyir| gnyis ka'i brjod bya thun mong bar[35] go bar mi nus te gnyis la 'tshams[36] sbyor ba'i thabs med pa'i phyir ro|| de 'ang[37] rnam 'grel las|

re re dag dang 'brel na ni||
don cig[38] mngon zhen bdag nyid can||
'chad po nyan po'i sems dag gi||
'tshams[39] sbyor bar ni mi 'gyur ro* zhes gsungs pa ltar ro||

gang zag so so la yod pa'i||
sems kyi rnam pa gnyis 'dra bas||
'dra la cig[40] tu zhen pa la||
tha snyad sbyor phyir mi 'gal na|| /7cd–8ab/

'chad nyan byed pa'i gang zag gnyis kyi don spyi rang rang gi blo dang 'brel yang lto ldir zhabs zhum pa la stsogs[41] pa'i rnam pa 'dra bas| 'dra ba la gcig tu zhen nas tha snyad 'dogs pa mi 'gal lo zhe na| ma yin te|

rang la shar na rang yul yin||
ma shar na ni de yul min||
des na tha dad bzung pa[42] la||
cig[43] tu 'dzin pa ga la srid|| /8cd–9ab/

blo la shar na gang zag rang rang gi blo dang rjes su 'brel pa'i spyi ni rang rang gi yul yin pas thun mong du mi 'dzin la| blo la ma shar na yul nyid ma yin pas phan tshun 'dra bar mi shes pa'i phyir don go ba mi srid do||

* PV III 337: nityam ātmani sambandhe pratīyāt kathitaṃ ca na | ekā ekena abhisambandhe pratisandhir na yujyate ||

[34] T1, T2: brjod

[35] T1, T2: ba

[36] T2: mtshams

[37] T1, T2: yang

[38] T1, T2: gcig

[39] T2: mtshams

[40] T1, T2: gcig

[41] T1, T2: sogs

[42] T1, T2: gzung ba

[43] T1, T2: gcig

Since a person explains solely that which is related to his own mind, then what is understood is that which is related to his own mind. That is why what is explained to both of them cannot be understood as being common. And this is because these two [people] are not interconnected in any way. Similarly, it is also said in *Pramāṇavārttika*:

> If each one is related to them, there is conviction that the object is the same.[21] [But] the minds of the explainer and the listener are not interconnected.[22]

> *Because the two aspects in the mind of each person are similar, these similarities can be conceived as one and the same. Since this is conventional connection, there is no contradiction.* /7cd–8ab/

Even though in the case of a person who does the exposition and a person who listens the object universal is related to one's own mind, then because such aspects as a vase's belly, spout, etc., are similar, there is no contradiction in applying conventions when you conceive what is similar as one and the same, they say. It is not like that, [says Sa skya Paṇḍita:]

> *If they emerge in oneself individually, they are one's own individual objects. If they do not emerge, they are not objects. Therefore, how is it possible to apprehend as one and the same those* [objects] *that were apprehended as different?* /8cd–9ab/

If they emerge in the mind, they will not be apprehended as common because the universality[23] related to one's own mind is one's own object. If they do not emerge in the mind, they are not the very objects. And that is why, since they are not cognized as mutually similar, it is not possible to understand the [very same] entity.[24]

tha dad yin yang yul cig[44] *tu||*
'khrul pa'i sgo nas 'dzin ce[45] *na||* /9cd/

don spyi rang rang gi yul tha dad yin yang 'khrul nas gcig du[46] 'dzin pas mi 'gal lo ce[47] na|

cig[48] *tu 'dzin pa 'khrul pa'i phyir||*
gzung yul med par grub pa yin|| /10ab/

don spyi yul gcig med pa la gcig tu rtog[49] pas bzung pa[50] yin pas rtog pa thams cad snang yul med pa nyid grub ste| rnam 'grel las|

gal te 'dra la de gcig par||
tha dad yod na de snang min||
tha dad bdag nyid ji ltar <3b> gzung||
de tshe blo don med can 'gyur* zhes gsungs pas so||

rigs pas brtags na med bzhin du||
da dung phal cher yul du zhe na||
sor mo'i rtse mos bstan pa na||
nam mkha' mthong zhes blun po 'khrul|| /10cd–11ab/

bar skabs kyi tshigs su bcad pa'o||

[2.2. rang gi 'dod pa brjod pa]

gnyis pa rang gi 'dod pa brjod na|

gzhal bya rang mtshan gcig kho na|| /11c/

shes pa'i yul ni rang gi mtshan nyid gcig kho na yin pas| blang dor byed pa thams cad rang gi mtshan nyid yod med la 'jug gi don byed mi nus pa la dgos nus med pa'i phyir mi 'jug ste| rnam 'grel las|

---

* PV III 378: ekārthābhiniveśātmā pravaktṛśrotṛcetasoḥ | tad ekavyavahāraś cet sādṛśyād atadābhayoḥ||

[44] T1, T2: gcig

[45] T1, T2: zhe

[46] T2: tu

[47] T1, T2: zhe

[48] T1, T2: gcig

[49] T2: rtogs

[50] T1, T2: gzung ba

Even though they are different, from the point of view of erroneous [cognition], *they are apprehended as one, they say...* /9cd/

Even though object universal is one's own object that is different [for different people], through erroneous [cognition] it is apprehended as one. And that is why there is no contradiction, they say [and Sa skya Paṇḍita answers:]

Since apprehending as one is erroneous, it is established as a nonexistent apprehended object. /10ab/

Because the object universal which is not one and the same object is conceptualized as one and the same, then since it is something that is apprehended, then all conceptualizations are established as having no appearing object. In *Pramāṇavārttika* it is said:

> If in what is similar the different ones are as if one and the same, they are not appearing. How then one can apprehend different ones? At that time mind has no entity [to apprehend].[25]

To put it another way:

If one examines it reasonably, it is as if nonexistent. [However] *still one most likely apprehends an object. If the sky is pointed out with the tip of the finger, fools who are erroneous claim they see it.*[26] /10cd–11ab/

[2.2. Presentation of our own position]

The second part is presentation of our own position, namely:

The perceptible[27] *is the only one particular.*[28] /11c/

Since the object of cognition is the only one particular, every act of acceptance and rejection is engaged in the particular regarding its existence or nonexistence. But it will not engage in what is not effective,[29] since it cannot be useful. So it is said in *Pramāṇavārttika*:

rang gi mtshid[51] gcig gzhal bya||
yod med nyid du dpyod rnams kyi||
don bya de las grub phyir ro* zhes[52]

dang|

med pa gzhal bya ma yin phyir||
gcig nyid ce na kho bo 'ang 'dod** ces gsungs pas so||

rang mtshan de nyid dngos su 'jal na gzung yul yin la| lkog gyur 'jal na zhen yul yin zhing| gnyis[53] ga yang skyes bus 'jug na mi slu[54] bas 'jug yul yin no||

[2.3. rtsod pa spang pa]
gsum pa rtsod pa spang pa[55] la gnyis te| [2.3.1] 'khrul shes yul med la rtsod pa spang pa[56] dang| [2.3.2] gzung yul rang mtshan la rtsod pa spang pa'o[57]||

[2.3.1. 'khrul shes yul med la rtsod pa spang pa]
dang po la bzhi las|

[2.3.1.1. gzhal bya gnyis su gsungs pa dang 'gal ba spang pa]
gzhal bya gnyis su gsungs pa dang 'gal ba spang ba ni|

yul gnyis bzhed pas gnod ce na|| /11d/

don spyi yul ma yin na bdag nyid chen po phyogs kyi glang pos gzhal bya gnyis su gsungs pa dang 'gal lo ce[58] na|

'jug tshul sgo nas rang spyi gnyis|| /12a/

---

* PV III 53d–54ab: ayaṃ meyaṃ tv ekaṃ svalakṣaṇam || tasmād arthakriyāsiddheḥ sadasattāvicāraṇāt |

** PV III 64cd: ekam eva aprameyatvād asataś cen mataṃ ca naḥ ||

51 T1, T2: mtshan nyid

52 T1, T2: zhes bya ba

53 T1, T2: gnyi

54 T1, T2: bslu

55 T1, T2: ba

56 T2: ba

57 T1, T2: ba'o

58 T1, T2: zhe

> Particular only [is] the perceptible, because those who analyze in terms of existence and nonexistence establish from it that which is to be effective.[30]

And

> since nonexistent is not the perceptible, I also maintain that there is one [object] alone.[31]

If one thoroughly perceives this very particular, it is the apprehended object.[32] If one perceives the indirect,[33] it is the conceived object.[34] And if somebody is engaged in both as well, then since they are non-deceptive they are objects of engagement be cause of non-deceptivness.

[2.3. Rebuttal of objections]
The third part is rebuttal of objections in two parts:

> [2.3.1] Rebuttal of the objection to the nonexistent object of erroneous cognition and
> [2.3.2] Rebuttal of the objection to the apprehended object as a particular.

[2.3.1. Rebuttal of the objection to the nonexistent object of erroneous cognition]
In the first there are four:

[2.3.1.1. Rebuttal of the contradiction with the statement that there are two perceptibles]
The rebuttal of the contradiction with the statement [of Dignāga] that there are two perceptibles is the following:

> *Accepting two objects* [by Dignāga] *invalidates* [your position],[35] *they say...* /11d/

If object universal is not an object, it contradicts great lord Dignāga's statement that there are two perceptibles,[36] they say [and Sa skya Paṇḍita answers:]

> *From the point of view of the way of engagement there are two: particular and* [object] *universal.* /12a/

gzhal bya gnyis yod nas gnyis su gsungs pa ma yin gyi| 'jal tshul kyi[59] sgo nas mngon gyur gyi[60] rang mtshan rang gis 'jal ba dang| lkog gyur gyi rang mtshan gzhal las 'jal ba la dgongs nas gnyis su gsungs pa yin te| rnam 'grel las

de ni rang gzhan ngo bo yis||
rtogs phyir gzhal bya gnyis su bzhed* ces bya ba dang|

gzhal bya gnyis phyir tshad ma gnyis||
don byed nus dang mi nus phyir** ces[61] gsungs pa ltar ro||

[2.3.1.2. don spyi dang med pa gsal ba yul du mtshungs pa'i rtsod pa spang pa]
gnyis pa don spyi dang med pa gsal ba yul du mtshungs pa'i rtsod pa <4a> spang pa[62] ni||

med pa 'ang gzhal byar mtshungs ce[63] *na*|| /12b/

kha gcig don spyi dang med pa gsal ba gnyis ka yul ma yin par mtshungs ba[64] la blo'i 'jug tshul gyis[65] don spyi gzhal byar 'jog pa ltar rtog med 'khrul pa'i dmigs pa de 'ang yul gsum par ci'i phyir mi 'gyur ce[66] na|

de la yul gyis[67] *dgos nus med*|| /12c/

skra shad la rtsogs[68] pa| phyi rol na yul dngos po la 'ang med| yul du zhen pa'ang med| zhen pa byas kyang don dang phrad pa'ang med| gal te phrang[69] na de 'jal gyi tshad ma gsum pa'ang[70] dgos pas yul gsum pa de lta bu mi srid do|| don spyi yul ma yin yang 'khrul nas zhugs pa na 'jug yul thob par nus pas yul du 'jog

---

* PV III 54cd: tasya svapararūpābhyāṃ gater meyadvayaṃ matam||
** PV III 1ab: mānaṃ dvividhaṃ meyadvaividhyāt śaktyaśaktitaḥ|
[59] T1, T2: gyi
[60] T2: gya
[61] T1, T2: zhes
[62] T1, T2: ba
[63] T1, T2: she
[64] T1, T2: pa
[65] T1, T2: gyi
[66] T1, T2: zhe
[67] T2: gyi
[68] T1, T2: sogs
[69] T2: phrad
[70] T2: la'ang

[Dignāga] didn't say that there are two because of the existence of the two. But he said that there are two, intending that from the point of view of the way of perceiving: direct particular perceived by it [cognition] and the indirect particular perceived through a different [object]. Similarly, it is said in *Pramāṇavārttika*:

> In that case, the two perceptibles are accepted because of realization by way of the nature of the [object] itself and the other [object].[37]

And

> since there are the two perceptibles, there are two valid cognitions, because there are the ones that are effective and the ones that are not.[38]

[2.3.1.2. Rebuttal of the objection that object universal and nonexistent clearly (appearing) are similar objects]

The rebuttal of the objection that object universal and nonexistent clearly [appearing] are similar objects is the following:

> *Even nonexistent is similar to the perceptible, they say...* /12b/

Concerning similarity in not being an object between object universal and nonexistent clearly [appearing], as when object universal into which mind is engaged is determined as perceptible, why not have also that which is erroneously perceived nonconceptually as the third object?, they say [and Sa skya Paṇḍita answers:]

> *In this case there can't be any purpose for that object.* /12c/

Such outer objects as a strand of hair, etc., do not even exist as a thing; there is not even conceiving of the object. Despite the act of conceiving, there is not even an encountering of an entity.[39] If there were an encountering, then there would be the need for a third [type] of valid cognition perceiving it as well; therefore the third object like that is not possible.

If there is an engagement while being erroneous even though object universal is not an object, then because of possibility of obtaining the object of engagement, [object universal] is included into [the category] of object; how then can it

pa'i phyir ga la mtshungs| 'o na rab rib can la skra shad la stsogs[71] par snang pa[72] 'di don byed mi nus pas don rang mtshan yang ma yin rtog pas ma bzung pas[73] spyi mtshan yang ma yin pas gang du 'du ce[74] na|

skra sogs snang pa[75] *blo nyid yin||*
skrar snang don la grub pa med||
de ni dngos por yod med ces||
rtog pas dpyod na spyi mtshan yin|| /12d–13ac/

skra shad 'dzin pa'i yul can ni shes pa nyid yin pas rang gi mtshan nyid las ma 'das so|| skrar snang yul du rlom pa ni gzhi med la 'khrul pas yul ci 'ang med pa nyid yin no|| skrar snang de dngos po yin nam dngos med yin ces[76] dpyod na rtog pa'i yul yin pas spyi'i khongs su 'du'o|| de'ang rnam 'grel las

skra shad la sogs don min te||
don du mos pa med phyir ro* zhes bya ba dang|

skra shad la sogs spyi min te||
don du zhen pa med phyir ro** zhes bya ba dang|

de dag gi yang de lta'i dngos||
bkag med gsal bar snang ba nyid||
shes pa'i ngo bo don nyid phyir||
skra sogs zhes bya'i blo dag ni||
spyi'i[77] spyod yul can yin la||
skrar snang don med can yin no*** zhes bya ba la sogs pa rgyas par gsungs so||

---

* PV III 1cd: arthakriyāyāṃ keśādirn na artho anarthādhimokṣataḥ ||

** PV III 7ab: keśādayo na sāmānyam arthānabhiniveśataḥ |

*** PV III 8–9ab: teṣām api tathābhāve apratiṣedhāt sphuṭābhatā | jñānarūpatayā arthatvāt keśādi iti matiḥ punaḥ || sāmānyaviṣayā keśapratibhāsam anarthakam |

[71] T1, T2: sogs

[72] T1, T2: ba

[73] T1, T2: bas

[74] T1, T2: zhe

[75] T1, T2: ba

[76] T1, T2: zhes

[77] T2: spyi yi

be similar [to the nonexistent clearly appearing]? Well then, since what appears to somebody with vitreus floaters as a strand of hair, etc.:

- is not effective, so it is neither an entity that is a particular,
- nor it is universal, since is not apprehended by conceptualization,

where to include it, they say [and Sa skya Paṇḍita answers:]

Appearances such as [a strand of] *hair etc. are mind itself. Appearance* [in the form] *of a hair is not established as an entity. So if to analyze conceptually whether it exists as a thing or does not exist, it is universal.* /12d–13ac/

Subject apprehending strand of hair is cognition itself, so it [cognition] does not go beyond its own characteristics. Concerning misinterpretation of the appearance of hair as an object, it does not exist as object whatsoever, because of the error due to the lack of a basis. If analyzing whether this appearance of the hair is a thing or non-thing, then since it is the object of conceptualization, it is categorized as universality. Because of that *Pramāṇavārttika* says extensively:

> The strands of hair etc. are not entities, since they are not intended as entities.[40]

And

> strand of hair, etc., are not universality, since they are not conceived as entities.[41]

And

> Things like the ones [mentioned] appear clearly without hindrances because they are of the very nature of cognition. States of mind such as the so called strand of hair, etc., have universals as [their] object of reference. The appearance of hair has no entity.[42]

[2.3.1.3. myong ba dang 'gal ba spang pa]

gsum pa myong ba dang 'gal ba spang pa[78] ni|

dngos med gnyis po rang rig gi||
shugs las grub pas bsal[79] *ce*[80] *na||* /13d–14a/

don spyi dang med pa gsal ba gnyis <4b> yul med pa yin na myong pas[81] grub pa ji ltar dgag ce na||

'khrul shes gnyis la yul med cing||
rang rig gis ni myong pa'i[82] *phyir||*
shes pa nyid yin de 'ang[83] *ni||*
med pa 'dzin phyir 'khrul shes yin|| /14b–15a/

yul du byas na gnod pa can gyi tshad ma yod pas| skra shad dang don spyi snang pa[84] de ni shes pa 'khrul ba[85] nyid yin te| de 'ang rnam 'grel las|

rung yul[86] gnas pas mi shes pa||
rang nyid shes phyir de shes yin* ces[87] dang

gal te spyi ni[88] shes ngo bos||
don nyid yin na thal bar 'gyur||
de ltar 'dod phyir skyon yod min** ces[89] gsungs pa ltar ro||

---

* PV III 16bc: na jñānaṃ tadyogyadeśakaiḥ | ajñātasya svayaṃ jñānān
** PV III 9c–10a: jñānarūpatayā arthatve sāmānye cet prasajyate || tatheṣṭatvād adoṣo
78 T1, T2: ba
79 T1, T2: gsal
80 T1, T2: zhe
81 T1, T2: bas
82 T1, T2: ba'i
83 T1, T2: yang
84 T1, T2: ba
85 T1, T2: pa
86 T1, T2: yul rung
87 T1, T2: zhes bya ba
88 T1, T2: yang
89 T1, T2: zhes

[2.3.1.3. Rebuttal of what contradicts the experience]
The rebuttal of what contradicts the experience is the following:

> *Both non-things are established with the help of self-knowing and that is why they are clear, they say...* /13d–14a/

If object universal and nonexistent clearly [appearing] are without an object, how to negate that they are established by experience, they say [and Sa skya Paṇḍita answers:]

> *Both erroneous cognitions have no object and because they are experienced by self-knowing, they are cognitions themselves. Moreover they are erroneous cognitions, because of apprehending non-being.* /14b–15a/

If you make [them] into an object, there is valid cognition invalidating it and that is why these appearances of a strand of hair and object universal are erroneous cognitions indeed.[43] Furthermore, as *Pramāṇavārttika* says:

> [It] is not cognized by way of positing a possible object. Because of self-cognizing itself it is cognition.[44]

And

> If also universality, being of the nature of cognition, is entity itself, there would be [the paradoxical] conclusion.[45] Since we assert it is just like this, there is no fault.[46]

[2.3.1.4. dgag pa tshad mas mi rtogs par thal ba spang ba]
bzhi pa dgag pa tshad mas mi rtogs par thal ba spang ba ni|

rang mtshan min pa'i yul med phyir[90]||
dngos med gzhal byar 'gal ce[91] *na*|| /15bc/

don rang gi mtshan nyid las gzhan pa'i gzhal bya med na| dngos med 'jal pa'i tshad ma mi srid par 'gyur ro ce[92] na|

dgag bya dngos por yod med ces||
sgrub[93] *pa'i phyir*[94] *'gal ba med*|| /15d–16a/

sgrub[95] na dngos por yod ces sgrub la| 'gog na dngos por med ces 'gog pa'i phyir te| de 'ang rnam 'grel las|

sgra don bsnyon pa med rnams kyi[96]||
yod med phyogs kyi bye brag gis||
dngos po nyid ni dpyad bya ste||
'di las 'bras 'byung rag las phyir||
don byed nus pa ma yin la||
don gnyer brtags pas ci zhig bya||
ma ning gzugs bzang mi bzang zhes||
'dod ldan rnams kyis brtags[97] ci phan* ces[98] gsungs pa ltar ro||

[2.3.2. gzung yul rang mtshan la rtsod pa spang ba]
gnyis pa gzung yul rang mtshan la rtsod pa spang ba la gnyis las

---

* PV I 210–211: sadasatpakṣabhedena śabdārthānapavādibhiḥ | vastv eva cintyate hy atra pratibaddhaḥ phalodayaḥ || arthakriyāsamarthasya vicāraiḥ kiṃ tadarthinām | ṣaṇḍhasya rūpavairūpye kāminyāḥ kiṃ parīkṣayā ||

[90] T1, T2: na
[91] T1, T2: zhe
[92] T1, T2: zhe
[93] T1, T2: bsgrub
[94] T1, T2: phyir na
[95] T1, T2: bsgrub
[96] T1, T2: kyis
[97] T1, T2: brtag
[98] T1, T2: zhes

[2.3.1.4. The rebuttal of the (paradoxical) conclusion of the negation being not realized by valid cognition]

The rebuttal of the [paradoxical] conclusion of the negation being not realized by valid cognition is the following:

> *If there is no object that is a particular, the non-thing contradicts the perceptible, they say...* /15bc/

If there is no perceptible which is different from the entity that is the very particular, valid cognition perceiving the non-thing will not be possible, they say [and Sa skya Paṇḍita answers:]

> *Since you establish whether what is to be negated is the existing or nonexisting thing, there is no contradiction.* /15d–16a/

This is because if you establish, you establish by [saying] "it exists as a thing" and if you negate, you negate by [saying] "it does not exist as a thing." So it is said in *Pramāṇavārttika*:

> When the ones who follow non-erroneous word and meaning analyze in terms of existence and nonexistence, there is the very thing to be analyzed, since the arising of the result depends on it.[47] Why should one investigate that which is not effective? What is the benefit for a lustful one in investigating whether an androgynous one is beautiful or not[48]?[49]

[2.3.2. Rebuttal of the objection concerning apprehended object as a particular]

Rebuttal of the objection concerning apprehended object as a particular in two parts.

[2.3.2.1. rtsod pa dgod pa]
dang po rtsod pa dgod na|

phyi'i[99] *gsung yul mkhas pas bkag*||
shes pa'i gzung yul 'dir mi srid||
des na gzhal bya gcig nyid kyang||
mi 'thad ces ni 'ga' zhig smra|| || /16b–17a/

gzung yul rang gi mtshan nyid de phyi rol gyi don yin na slob dpon gyis bkag la rang rig pa yin na yul du 'gal lo ce'o[100]||

[2.3.2.2. lan]
gnyis pa lan la gsum las

[2.3.2.2.1. grub mtha'i rnam gzhag spyir dpyad pa]
dang po grub mtha'i rnam gzhag spyir dpyad na|

ngo bo nyid dang dbang phyug dang|| <5a>
gtso bo rdul dang rnam rig dang||
rten 'brel yin zhes grub pa'i mtha'||
tha dad rang bzhan sde pa 'dod|| /17b–18a/

mu steg byed ngo bo nyid rgyur smra ba ni| thams cad ngo bo nyid las byung ba dang| dbang phyug pa dbang phyug gis byas pa dang| grangs can gtso bos byas pa dang| gzegs zan dang nyan thos rdul phran gyis byas pa dang| sems tsam pa sems dang| dbu ma 'ang[101] don dam par spros pa dang bral zhing kun rdzob du dngos por smra ba dag[102] gi rjes su 'jug kyang rung| 'jig rten grags sde dang bstun yang rung ste| de dag gang ltar yang kun tu tha snyad pa la don dang shes pa gnyis su kha tshon chod do|

[2.3.2.2.2. gzhan gyis brtags pa dgag pa]
gnyis pa de la gzhan gyis brtags pa dgag na| ngo bo nyid rgyur smra ba ni rgyu med las skyes[103] ba yin pas|

---

[99] T1: phyi yi
[100] T1, T2: zhe'o
[101] T1, T2: pa'ng
[102] T1, T2: de dag
[103] T1, T2: skye

[2.3.2.1. Determining the objection]
Determining the objection:

> *Some claim that the outer apprehended object was negated by the wise man. This* [kind of] *apprehended object of cognition is not possible. Therefore not even one perceptible is accepted.* /16b–17a/

If an apprehended object as a particular would be an outer entity, ācārya negated it.[50] If it is self-knowing, it contradicts the object,[51] they say.

[2.3.2.2. Answer]
The answer [of Sa skya Paṇḍita] has three points.

[2.3.2.2.1. Analysis of the general presentation of tenet system]
Analysis of the general presentation of tenet system:

> *Our and other groups*[52] *claim different tenets saying it is: nature, Almighty*[53]*, The Principal One*[54]*, atoms, knowledge through the aspect*[55] *and coemergent arising.* /17b–18a/

Tīrthikas claim that the cause is nature; everything arises from nature.[56] According to Śivaists creation is due to Śiva; according to Sāṃkhya creation is due to Viṣṇu; according to Leftovers eaters[57] and Śrāvakas creation is due to atoms. According to Cittamātrins due to the mind. And according to Mādhyamikas, either it is correct to follow the claim that it is ultimately free from elaborations and that things are of completely obscured [truth],[58] or it is correct to agree with the common opinions of the world.[59] They determine that whatever is completely conventional is finally [either] an entity [or] cognition.[60]

[2.3.2.2.2. Refutation of others' theories]
Refutation of others' theories: In the case of the proponents of nature as the cause, it is [in fact] generated without cause.[61] Therefore:

rgyu med gzhan la mi ltos phyir||
rtag tu yod pa 'am med par 'gyur* ces[104] pas khegs la|

dbang phyug dang| gtso bo gnyis ka'ang rtag pa byed pa por 'gal bas mi 'thad do||

[2.3.2.2.3. bde bar gshegs pa'i lugs bsgrub pa]
gsum pa bde bar gshegs pa'i lugs bsgrub pa la gnyis las|

[2.3.2.2.3.1. dgongs pa ngos gzung pa]
dang po dgongs pa ngos gzung[105] pa ni thub pas phyi rol dpyod pa na rdul phran zhal gyis bzhes la| tha snyad kyi de kho na dpyod pa na sems[106] zhal gyis bzhes shing| don dam pa'i de kho na nyid la 'jug pa na spros pa dang bral ba la 'jug par mdzad do| de 'ang rnam 'grel las|

des de nyid don btang snyems can||
glang chen gzigs stangs nyid mdzad nas||
'jig rten thugs ni 'ba' zhig gis||
phyi rol dpyod la 'jug par mdzad** ces bya ba la sogs pa gsungs pa ltar ro|

[2.3.2.2.3.2. slob dpon gyis ji ltar gtan la phab pa'i tshul]
gnyis pa de slob dpon gyis ji ltar gtan la phab pa'i tshul la| [2.3.2.2.3.2.1] don rig dang| [2.3.2.2.3.2.2] rnam rig gnyis so|

[2.3.2.2.3.2.1. don rig]
dang po la gsum ste| [2.3.2.2.3.2.1.1] gzhan lugs dgag| [2.3.2.2.3.2.1.2] rang lugs rjod[107]| [2.3.2.2.3.2.1.3] de la[108] rtsod pa spang pa'o|

[2.3.2.2.3.2.1.1. gzhan lugs dgag pa]
dang po la gnyis las thog mar [2.3.2.2.3.2.1.1.1] bye brag du[109] smra ba'i lugs dgag na|

---

* PV I 35ab: nityaṃ sattvam asattvaṃ vā 'hetor anyānapekṣaṇāt |

** PV III 219: tadupekṣitatattvārthaiḥ kṛtvā gajanimīlanam | kevalaṃ lokabuddhyā eva bāhyacintā pratanyate ||

[104] T1, T2: zhes

[105] T1, T2: bzung

[106] T1, T2: sems tsam

[107] T1, T2: brjod

[108] *de la* omitted in T1, T2.

[109] T1, T2: tu

> what is causeless is not interlinked with something else, and that is why it will either be permanently existent or nonexistent[62]

– saying so it is rebutted. Since for both Īśvara and Viṣṇu being permanent contradicts their being creators, they are not admissible.[63]

[2.3.2.2.3. Establishing the system of Sugata]
Establishing the system of Sugata in two parts.

[2.3.2.2.3.1. Identifying the intent]
Identifying the intent is the following: Muni proclaimed that if to investigate the outside [world], atoms are asserted; if to investigate the thatness of the conventional, the mind only is asserted; and if to consider thatness of the ultimate, freedom from elaborations is approached. *Pramāṇavārttika* also says like that:

> Therefore acting like an elephant looking at reality with indifference, [Buddha] engages in the investigation of the outer [world] solely with [this kind of] mind frame.[64]

[2.3.2.2.3.2. The way the ācārya settled the question]
Concerning the way the ācārya [Dignāga] settled the question, there are:
[2.3.2.2.3.2.1] knowledge of entity and
[2.3.2.2.3.2.2] knowledge through the aspect.[65]

[2.3.2.2.3.2.1. Knowledge of entity]
It the first one there are three parts:
[2.3.2.2.3.2.1.1] refutation of other systems,
[2.3.2.2.3.2.1.2] presentation of our system,
[2.3.2.2.3.2.1.3] rebuttal of objections.

[2.3.2.2.3.2.1.1. Refutation of other systems]
It has two points: initially [2.3.2.2.3.2.1.1.1] the refutation of the Vaibhāṣika system.

[2.3.2.2.3.2.1.1.1. bye brag du smra ba'i lugs dgag pa]

chod pa min phyir rnam shes min||
dbang po sten[110] *bcas lta byed lo*|| /18bc/

bye brag du[111] smra ba na re rnam shes kyis[112] don 'dzin na chod pa'i gzugs <5b> kyang mthong bar thal bas| de mtshungs gyi[113] dbang po 'dzin byed ma yin yang sten[114] bcas kyi dbang po lta byed yin no zhes zer ro|| 'di mi 'thad de|

bems po yin phyir lta byed min||
dus mnyam pa la 'brel pa med|| /18d–19a/

dbang po bems po yin pas lta byed du mi 'thad la| yul dang yul can dus mnyam pa la 'brel pa gnyis ka mi 'thad pa'i phyir ro||

[2.3.2.2.3.2.1.1.2. bod kyi lugs dgag pa]
gnis pa bod kyi lugs dgag na|

yul dang rnam shes dus mnyam ni||
gzung 'dzin yin zhes gangs can pa|| /19bc/

bod phal cher ni| dus mi mnyam na yul du mi rung zhing dbang po lta byed ma yin pas dus mnyam pa'i yul dang rnam shes gzung 'dzin yin zhes smra'o|| 'di'ang mi 'thad de|

dus mnyam phyir na 'brel pa med||
rgyu med pa la rnam shes 'gal|| /19d–20a/

yul dang rnam shes dus mnyam pa 'brel pa med pas mi 'dzin la| yul rgyu ma yin na don rig gi rnam shes dmigs pa'i rgyu med las skye bar 'gyur ro||

skad cig snga ma'i yul rgyu yin|
dus mnyam gzung yul yin ce[115] *na*|| /20bc/

[110] T1, T2: rten
[111] T1, T2: tu
[112] T2: kyi
[113] T1: kyi; T2: kyis
[114] T1, T2: rten
[115] T1, T2: zhe

[2.3.2.2.3.2.1.1.1. Refutation of the Vaibhāṣika system]

> *Since* [object] *is not the indirect one*[66], *it is not consciousness* [that perceives it]. *The sense faculty with support*[67] *would be the one that sees.* /18bc/

Vaibhāṣika says "if the consciousness apprehends the entity, it follows that even the indirect one would be seen. That is why passive sense faculty is not the one that apprehends, but sense faculty with support is that which sees."[68] This is not acceptable.

> *Since* [the sense faculty] *is matter, it is not the one which sees. There is no relation between the simultaneous ones.* /18d–19a/

Since the sense faculty is matter, it is not acceptable as the one which sees. It is also because it is not acceptable that simultaneous object and subject are related in two ways.[69]

[2.3.2.2.3.2.1.1.2. Refutation of Tibetan systems]
Refutation of Tibetan systems:

> *The ones from the Land of Snow say that simultaneous object and consciousness are the apprehended one and the apprehender.* /19bc/

The majority of Tibetans asserts that there can't be an object which is not simultaneous [with consciousness] and that the sense faculty is not the one that sees.[70] And that is why simultaneous object and consciousness are the apprehended and the apprehender. This is also not acceptable.

> *Because of simultaneity there is no relation. Consciousness contradicts that which is without cause.*[71] /19d–20a/

Since there is no relation between the simultaneous object and consciousness, it is not apprehended. If the object is not a cause, the consciousness knowing the entity will be generated without the cause for seeing.

> *The cause is the object* [which is] *one moment earlier. It is the object apprehended simultaneously, they say...* /20bc/

skad gcig gis snga ba'i[116] yul rnam shes kyi dmigs pa'i rgyu yin la|| dus mnyam pa'i yul gzung yul yin no ce[117] na|

yul las skyes phyir rnam shes grub||
de la dus mnyam dgos pa med|| /20d-21a/

skad gcig gis snga ba'i[118] yul dang| dbang po dang| yid la byed pa las skyes ba[119] de nyid kyis rnam shes grub mod| de las gzhan pa'i dus mnyam pa'i yul ci zhig dgos|| rnam shes rgyu las skye'ang dus mnyam pa'i yul re grogs su dgos na dus mnyam pa'i dbang po la sogs pa'ang grogs su dgos pas ha cang thal te| ma la yar rgyu tshogs pa las tsan d+han[120] skye 'ang gangs can gyi ri grogs su dgos so zhes smra ba bzhin no des na rnam 'grel las|

rgyu'i[121] dngos po[122] ma gtogs pa'i||
gzung ba zhes bya ci 'ang med[123] ces ba[124] dang||

rnam nges las kyang|

rnam pa gtod par nus pa'i phyir shes pa'i yul ni rgyu yin la rjes su 'gro ba dang ldog pa'i rjes su mi byed pa ni rgyu ma yin zhing| rgyu ma yin pa ni yul ma yin no[*] zhes <6a> gsungs pa ltar ro||

bde bar gshegs pas kyang|

mig la brten cing gzugs la dmigs nas mig gi rnam par shes pa skye zhes gsungs pa'ang de yin no||

[2.3.2.2.3.2.1.2. rang lugs rjod pa]
gnyis pa rang 'dod pa ni| phyi rol gyi don khas len pa na mdo sde pa'i lugs gzung bar bya'o||

---

[*] PVin I 15.
[116] T1, T2: ma'i
[117] T1, T2: zhe
[118] T1, T2: ma'i
[119] T1, T2: pa
[120] T1, T2: tsan+dan [candana]
[121] T1, T2: rgyu yi
[122] T1, T2: ngo bo
[123] PV III 224 ab: hetubhāvād ṛte na anyā grāhyatā nāma kācana |
[124] T1, T2: ces bya ba

The object that is one moment earlier is the cause for seeing by consciousness and the simultaneous object is the apprehended object, they say [and Sa skya Paṇḍita answers:]

> *Consciousness is established because it is generated from the object. There is no need for being simultaneous with it.* /20d–21a/

Consciousness is established the very generation from the object, the sense faculty, and the mental focusing one moment earlier.[72] What would the simultaneous object that is other from them be needed for? If consciousness is generated from the cause and must accompany every simultaneous object, then because of the need for a simultaneous sense faculty accompanying it, there would be a [paradoxical] consequence going much too far. It would be similar to saying that even though in Mount Malaya[73] sandalwood is generated from a group of causes, it would need to be accompanied by the mountains of the Land of Snow.[74] Therefore *Pramāṇavārttika* says:

> Except the thing which is the cause there is nothing so called apprehended whatsoever.[75]

And *Pramanaviniścaya* says as well similarly:

> Because of having the ability to reveal [its] aspect, the object of consciousness is a cause. What does not function by way of positive concomitance and reverse one is not the cause, and what is not a cause is not an object.[76]

Such are also the words of Sugata:

> With the eye as the basis and because of perceiving the form, the eye-consciousness is generated.[77]

[2.3.2.2.3.2.1.2. Presentation of our system]

Our position is as follows: if you accept outer entity, you should maintain the system of Sautrāntika.

yul dang dbang po yid la byed||
de las skyes pa[125] *rnam shes yin*|| /21bc/

yul dang dbang po dang yid la byed pa tshogs pa'i skad gcig[126] dang po de nyid phyi rol gyi don bems po 'dra ba'i skyed byed yin la| de dag tshogs pa las skad gcig[127] gnyis par rnam shes phyi rol yul gyi rnam pa 'dra bar skyes pa de nyid skyes la 'dra ba'i shes pa yin no|| de gnyis rgyu 'bras yin pas gzung 'dzin dus mi mnyam mo|| 'o na shes pa'i rgyu yin par thams cad mtshungs pa la shes pa yul kho na dang 'dra bar skye la| dbang po la sogs pa dang 'dra bar mi skye ba ci yin ce[128] na| de dngos po'i chos nyid yin te|

zas sogs bu'i[129] *rgyu yin yang*||
pha ma'i zugs[130] *bzhin yul 'drar skye*|| /21d–22a/

bu'i rgyu zas dang dus dang drod la sogs pa yin yang pha ma'i dbyibs dang 'dra'i gzhan gyi ma yin pa bzhin no|| de yang rnam 'grel las|

dper na zas dang dus la sogs||
bu skye ba'i[131] rgyu yin yang||
de ni pha ma gcig gi gzugs||
'dzin 'gyur gzhan 'ga'i ma yin bzhin* ces[132] gsungs pa ltar ro||

des na yul la 'bras bu gnyis|| /22b/

dper na yul bum pa lta bu la khos nyer len gyi rgyu byas pa'i bum pa'i skad gcig[133] gnyis pa bems por skyed pa dang| dbang po'i grogs byas nas mig gi rnam par shes pa gzugs dang 'dra bar skye ba ste lag rjes gnyis skyed pa yin no||

blo 'ang tshul gnyis yin par 'dod|| /22c/

* PV III 369: yathā eva āhārakālāder hetutve apatyajanmani | pitros tad ekasya ākāraṃ dhatte na anyasya kasyacit ||

[125] T1, T2: pa'i
[126] T1, T2: cig
[127] T1, T2: cig
[128] T1, T2: zhe
[129] T1, T2: bu yi
[130] T1, T2: gzugs
[131] T1, T2: ba yi
[132] T1, T2: zhes
[133] T1, T2: cig

It is consciousness generated from object, sense faculty and mental focusing. /21bc/

The very first moment of collecting together object, sense faculty and mental focusing are generators of outer entity similar to matter. Just after collecting them, in the second moment the consciousness which is generated as similar to the aspect of outer object is the cognition similar to that what was generated.[78] Since these two[79] are cause and effect, what is apprehended and apprehender are not simultaneous.[80]

Well then, all of them are like that which is a cause of cognition, so why cognition is generated as similar to the object only and not generated as similar to the sense faculties etc.? [Sa skya Paṇḍita answers:] Such is the nature of things and

Even though the nourishment etc. are causes of the child, its body is similar to that of the parents, so alike [cognition] *is generated as similar to the object.* /21d–22a/

Even though nourishment, time and warmth are causes of the child, its shape is similar to that of the parents. It is not like other ones. In the same way it is said in *Pramāṇavārttika*:

> For example even though nourishment, time etc. are the causes of child being born, it will take the form of parents' only. It is not like this other few.[81]

Therefore concerning the object there are two results. /22b/

It is, for example, like in the case of the object such as vase: [1] the second moment of vase that serves as a main cause[82] is generated by it [the vase] as matter, and [2] after being accompanied by sense faculty eye consciousness is generated as similar to the form. So are the two outcomes generated.

[We] *proclaim that mind as well is of two modes.* /22c/

yul shes pa'i blo dang blo de shes pa'i blo ste blo tshul gnyis pa yin no|| de nyid mdo las|

> yul shes de'i[134] shes pa'i[135]|| dbye bas blo ni tshul gnyis nyid ces bya ba dang|

rnam 'brel las|

> tshul gnyis dang ni rang rig grub||[*] ces gsungs ba[136] ltar ro||

[2.3.2.2.3.2.1.3. rtsod pa spang pa]
gsum pa rtsod pa spang pa[137] ni| bod rnams phyi rol gyi <6b> don lkog na mo zhes bya ba rnam par[138] 'jog byed gos gyi[139] lkog na lag pa yod pa lta bur bsams nas| phyi rol don gyis rnam pa bzhag na 'o na de las gzhan pa sha zas bzhag go zhes mgo sgre[140] ba ni mi mtshungs te| sha zas bzhag na shes pa sha za dang 'dra bar skye dgos la| bum pa la sogs pa la sha zar 'dogs na ming la mi brtsad do|| des na phyi rol gyi don khas len bzhin du mdo sde ba[141] 'gog pa ni chos kyi grags pa'i dgongs pa ma shes pa yin no|| chos kyi grags pa nyid kyis kyang| gal te phyi rol dpyod la 'jug pa na|| kho bos mdo sde'i skas la rnam par brten ces[142] gsungs par grag go||

[2.3.2.2.3.2.2. rnam rig]
gnyis pa rnam rig la gsum ste| [2.3.2.2.3.2.2.1] gzhan gyis brtags pa dgag pa| [2.3.2.2.3.2.2.2] rnam par rig pa bsgrub pa| [2.3.2.2.3.2.2.3] de la rtsod pa spang pa'o[143]||

[2.3.2.2.3.2.2.1. gzhan gyis brtags pa dgag pa]
dang po la gnyis las thob[144] mar

---

[*] PV III 371d: siddhe dvirūpatvātmavedane ||
[134] T1, T2: de yi
[135] T1, T2: pa yi
[136] T1, T2: pa
[137] T1, T2: ba
[138] T1, T2: pa
[139] T1, T2: kyi
[140] T1, T2: bsgre
[141] T1: mod sde pa
[142] T1, T2: zhes
[143] T1, T2: ba'o
[144] T1, T2: thog

The mind cognizing the object and the mind cognizing this mind are two modes of the mind. [*Tattvaprakāśa*]*sutra* says:

> Since there is division into cognition of the object and cognition of it [cognition of the object], there are two modes of mind.

Similarly, *Pramāṇavārttika* says:

> Self-knowing establishes two modes.[83]

[2.3.2.2.3.2.1.3. Rebuttal of objections]

Rebuttal of objections is the following: Tibetans think that the outer entity, which is the so called hidden, is like the hand being there hidden in the coat. And so if the aspect is posited by outer entity, well then, the analogous example of "being posited by the ghost different from it [the hidden]" will not be relevant.[84] If ghost posits it, there should be generation of cognition being similar to the ghost. If the vase etc. is called the ghost, I will not discuss this name.

That is why while accepting the outer object they refute Sautrāntika, which means that they do not know the intent of Dharmakīrti. However Dharmakīrti himself is known from saying: "If engaging in analysis of outer [object], I fully rely on the level of Sautrāntika."[85]

[2.3.2.2.3.2.2. Knowledge through the aspect]

Knowledge through the aspect in three [points]:

[2.3.2.2.3.2.2.1] refutation of investigation made by others,
[2.3.2.2.3.2.2.2] establishment of knowledge through the aspect,
[2.3.2.2.3.2.2.3] rebuttal of the objections to that.

[2.3.2.2.3.2.2.1. Refutation of investigation made by others]

In the first from the two the first [one is]:

[2.3.2.2.3.2.2.1.1. phyi rol gyi don grub pa dgag pa]
phyi rol gyi don grub pa dgag na|

cig[145] *dang du ma bral ba'i phyir*||
don med des na rnam pa'ang med|| /22d–23a/

yul rags[146] pa yan lag can gyi rdzas sam phra mo cha med kyi du mar brtags nas 'gog na bye brag pas khas blangs pa'i yan lag can gyi rdzas gcig med de| phyogs cha du ma dang 'brel ba'i[147] phyir 'bru'i phung po bzhin zhes bya bas khegs so|| phra mo cha med kyi du mar bden pa'ang mu stegs byed dang nyan thos kyis brtags pa'i rdul phran bden pa med de| cha drug dang 'brel pa'i phyir khang pa bzhin zhes bya bas khegs te| drug gis gcig car[148] sbyar bas[149] na|| phra rab rdul cha drug du[150] 'gyur|| drug po dag ni go gcig na|| gong bu'ang rdul phran tsam du 'gyur* zhes gsungs pa ltar ro|| yang rdul phran gcig dang gnyis mthud pa la ring thung yod med brtags pas kyang khegs so|| de nyid chos kyi grags pas|

ang gyis dngos po rnam dpyad na||
de nyid du na de dngos med||
gang gi phyir na de dag la||
cig[151] dang du ma'i rang bzhin med** ces gsungs pa ltar ro||

[2.3.2.2.3.2.2.1.2. 'jig rten grags pa la brten pa dgag pa]
gnyis pa 'jig rten <7a> grags pa la brten pa dgag na|

kun rdzob 'jig rten grags pa la||
brten na tshad ma'i rnam gzhag 'gal|| /23bc/

rtog ge ba kha gcig[152] slob dpon zla ba grags pa dang mthun par kun rdzob 'jig rten grags sde dang bstun nas 'jog la| de'ang gang zag 'jig rten pa ma yin gyi

---

* *Viṃśatikā* 12: ṣaṭkena yugapadayogāt paramāṇoḥ ṣaḍaṃśarā | ṣaṇṇāṃ samānadeśatvāt piṇḍaḥ syād aṇumātrakaḥ ||

** PV III 360 / PVin I 51: bhāvā yena nirūpyante tadrūpaṃ nāsti tattvatah | yasmād ekam anekaṃ vā rūpaṃ teṣāṃ na vidyate ||

145 T1, T2: gcig
146 T1, T2: yul la rags
147 T1, T2: pa'i
148 T1, T2: gcig char
149 T1, T2: ba
150 T2: tu
151 T1, T2: gcig
152 T1, T2: cig

[2.3.2.2.3.2.2.1.1. Refutation of outer entity]
If you refute establishment of outer entity [then]:

> *because of being free from the one and the many, entity does not exist and therefore the aspect does not exist either.* /22d–23a/

In case of the object if it is refuted by analyzing the matter that is gross and has parts or numerous partless subtle [particles], then there is no single matter with parts asserted by Vaiśeṣikas. Since [this substance] is related to many parts, it is rejected by [reasoning] called "the similar to the heap of grains."[86] Even though multiplicity of partless subtle [particles] is truly [existing], Tīrthikas and Śrāvakas reject them, saying that particles analyzed do not truly exist, since they are related to six parts, [and] they are similar to a house.[87] Similarly it is said:

> If six [atoms] were joined at once to one subtle atom,[88] it would have six parts. And if six were in one place, this mass would be one atom only.[89]

Also analyzing whether one particle joined to the other will be or will not be longer or shorter,[90] they reject it as well. Thus spoke Dharmakīrti:

> If somebody analyzes completely the thing, within suchness there is no thing. For that reason in their case there is no essence of the one and the many.[91]

[2.3.2.2.3.2.2.1.2. Refutation of relying on worldly opinions]
Refutation of relying on worldly opinions:

> *If to rely on worldly opinions which are completely obscured* [truth], *it contradicts presentation of valid cognition.* /23bc/

Some dialectician[92] says: "In accordance with Candrakīrti one posits completely obscured [truth] compatibly with worldly opinions. Furthermore [the ones meant

blo 'jig rten pa ma brtags ma dpyad par 'jug pa dang 'thun par 'jug go zhes zer ro|| 'di'ang kun du[153] tha snyad pa'i tshad ma dpyod pa na mi 'thad de| ma brtags pa'i blo ngor mngon sum dang rjes dpag dang sgrub pa dang gzhan sel la stsogs[154] pa mi 'jug pas tshad ma dang tshad ma ma yin pa'i rnam bzhag[155] sde bdun las bshad pa thams cad nub par 'gyur ro|| gal te 'jig rten grub mtha' khas len pa de dag gi rjes su 'brang par[156] 'dod na shes bya la dngos po dngos med gnyis| dngos po la bem[157] rig gnyis las ma 'das pas bems po'i lugs gang 'dod kyang bkag zin la| rig pa ni sems tsam pa las gzhan 'thad pa ma yin no||

[2.3.2.2.3.2.2.2. rnam par rig pa bsgrub pa]

gnyis pa rnam par rig pa bsgrub pa ni kun du[158] tha snyad pa'i tshad ma dpyod pa na mdo mdzad pa dang rnam 'grel mdzad pa'i rjes su 'brang ngo|| de la gnyis te|

> *gsal dang lhan gcig*[159] *dmigs pas 'grub*|| /23d/

[2.3.2.2.3.2.2.2.1. shes pa'i mtshan nyid]

dang po ni shes pa'i mtshid[160] gsal zhing rig pa yin la| gsal zhing rig pa dang mi ldan pa'i shes pa[161] mi srid pas shes bya thams cad sems su grub ste lkog shal gyis ba glang sgrub[162] pa bzhin no||

[2.3.2.2.3.2.2.2.2. lhan gcig dmigs nges kyis 'grub pa]

gnyis pa lhan gcig[163] dmigs nges kyis 'grub ste|

> *lhan gcig*[164] *dmigs la gzhan mi srid*||
> *rdzas gzhan yin na rtags mi srid*|
> *zla ba gnyis*[165] *snang bzhin sngo 'dzin yang*||
> *gzhan la mtha' gzhan bkag pas khegs*|| /24/

---

[153] T1, T2: tu
[154] T1, T2: sogs
[155] T1, T2: gzhag
[156] T1, T2: bar
[157] T1, T2: bems
[158] T1, T2: tu
[159] T1, T2: cig
[160] T1, T2: mtshan nyid
[161] T1, T2: bya
[162] T1, T2: lang bsgrub
[163] T1, T2: cig
[164] T1, T2: cig
[165] T1, T2: zla gnyis

here] are not persons who are worldly beings but they grasp in accordance with the worldly mind's way of grasping without examination and analysis." If also this is analyzed with completely conventional valid cognition, it is not admissible. So all explanation in seven treatises [of Dharmakīrti] presenting what is and what is not valid cognition, would be in vain, since from the perspective of mind that does not analyze you do not engage in perception, inference, proof, *apoha*. If you want to follow the worldly beings asserting tenet system,[93] in the case of the cognizable [objects] there are the two: thing and non-thing. In case of thing since there is nothing beyond the two: matter and knowledge, then even though you assert some materialistic system, it is already refuted. Concerning the knowledge, the other than mind only is not admissible.

[2.3.2.2.3.2.2.2. Establishment of knowledge through the aspect]
Establishment of knowledge through the aspect is as follows: In case of analyzing with completely conventional valid cognition, we follow the way of the Sutra [*Pramāṇasamuccaya*] and the way of *Pramāṇavārttika*. Here are two points:

> *Establishing through clear and concurrent perception.* /23d/

[2.3.2.2.3.2.2.2.1. Definition of consciousness]
Definition of consciousness is as follows: it is clear and knowing.[94] Cognizable [object] that does not have [the quality of] being clear and known is impossible. That is why all cognizable [objects] are established as the mind. Like the cow is established by dewlap.[95]

[2.3.2.2.3.2.2.2.2. Establishing by way of concurrent perception]
Establishing by way of concurrent perception is the following:

> *In* [the case of] *the concurrent perception something different* [from it] *is impossible. If there would be different substance, the reason would be impossible. It is like seeing two moons. Apprehending of the blue and the different* [object from it] *is rejected by negating different pole* [the object which is different].[96] /24/

'di la gsum las thog mar

[2.3.2.2.3.2.2.2.2.1. rtags dgod pa]
rtags dgod pa ni| gang lhan gcig[166] dmigs pas nges pa de gzhan ma yin te zla ba gnyis snang bzhin| sngon po dang de 'dzin gyi shes pa'ang lhan gcig[167] dmigs pas nges so zhes bya ba khyab byed 'gal ba dmigs pa'o| de'ang blo'i dngos po <7b> gcig gis dus gcig du[168] rtogs pas nges par nus pa'o|| de nyid lhan gcig[169] dmigs pas nges pa'i phyir|| sngo dang de blo gzhan ma yin[*] zhes gsungs pa ltar ro||[170]

[2.3.2.2.3.2.2.2.2.2. rtags de'i tshul bsgrub pa]
rtags de'i tshul bsgrub pa 'ang| phyogs chos ni rang rig gis grub la|| khyab pa 'ang dpe zla ba gnyis la stsogs[171] pa'i steng du 'grub cing| de mi mthun phyogs la 'gog pa 'ang| mi mthun phyogs dngos po tha dad dus mi mnyam pa la lhan gcig dmigs nges ni dus mi mnyam par 'dzin pa nyid kyis khegs la| dus mnyam pa la 'ang sgro btags pa ni[172] sgro btags par shes pa nyid kyis yul gzhan med par grub cing| rdzas tha dad dus mnyam pa la ni gnod pa can gyi rtags kyis khegs te| gang 'brel pa med pa de lhan gcig dmigs pas nges pa med de sngon po dang ser po bzhin| mig dang gzugs kyang rdzas tha dad dus mnyam par khyong[173] gyis khas blangs so zhe[174] pas khegs so||

[2.3.2.2.3.2.2.2.2.3. rtsod pa spang pa]
gsum pa rtsod pa spang pa[175] la gsum las

[2.3.2.2.3.2.2.2.2.3.1. btsun pa dge bsrungs la stsogs pa'i rtsod pa spang ba]
dang po ni btsun pa dge bsrungs la stsogs[176] pa dag rtags 'di ma grub ste gang zag du mas zla ba lta bu'i gzung pa[177] gcig la lta ba'i tshe rang rang gi 'dzin pa dmigs kyang gzhan gyi[178] ma dmigs so zhe na| gcig gi gzung ba gcig la dmigs pa

[*] PVin I 55 b.
[166] T1, T2: cig
[167] T1, T2: cig
[168] T1, T2: tu
[169] T1, T2: cig
[170] T1, T2: gnyis
[171] T1, T2: sogs
[172] T1, T2: btags ni
[173] T1, T2: khyed
[174] T1, T2: zhes
[175] T1, T2: ba
[176] T1, T2: sogs
[177] T1, T2: ba
[178] T1, T2: gyis

From among three points here first:

[2.3.2.2.3.2.2.2.2.1. Necessity of the reason]

The necessity of the reason: what is ascertained by concurrent perception is not different, like appearance of two moons. And also blue [color] and cognition that apprehends it are ascertained by concurrent perception. This way of putting it is [inference] of perception of contradiction with the pervader.[97] With regard to that they can be ascertained, since they are realized simultaneously by way of one thing which is mind. Since they are ascertained by concurrent perception, "blue [color] and the mind [cognizing] it are not different,"[98] as it is said.

[2.3.2.2.3.2.2.2.2.2. Establishment of the modes of this reason]

Establishment of the modes of this reason [*trairūpya*]:[99] The subject [*phyogs chos*] is established by self-knowing.[100] Pervasion as well is established on top of the examples of two moons etc.[101] Dissimilar class is negated. In a dissimilar class the thing different [from the mind] is not simultaneous; concerning ascertaining by concurrent perception, it is rejected by non-simultaneous apprehending. Concerning imputation also in case of simultaneity, the very understanding of imputation establishes that the object that is different [from it] does not exist. And a substance that is different and simultaneous is rejected with reason of invalidation[102]. There is no ascertainment by concurrent perception of something that is not related.[103] [I, Sa skya Paṇḍita] reject your declaration that the eye and the form – like blue and yellow color – are different and simultaneous substances.

[2.3.2.2.3.2.2.2.2.3. Rebuttal of the objections]

Rejecting the objections has three parts:

[2.3.2.2.3.2.2.2.2.3.1. Rebuttal of the objection of bTsun pa dGe bSrung and others]

bTsun pa dGe bSrung[104] and others say that "this reasoning is not established. When many persons see one apprehended [thing] like the moon, even though one's own apprehending [subject] perceives, the others do not perceive it." If [they say] so, [I, Sa skya Paṇḍita answer:] what one apprehended is not perceived as one and the same but is experienced according to similar karmic tendencies.

ma yin gyi las kyi bag chags 'thun par sad pa yin te| rmi lam gyi zla ba 'am[179] rab rib can rnams kyi[180] skra shad snang ba ltar skyon med do||

[2.3.2.2.3.2.2.2.2.3.2. rtags 'di 'gal ba spang ba]

gnyis pa rtags 'di 'gal te| lhan gcig[181] la gnyis kyis khyab pas rtags don gzhan du med pa las bzlog pas khyab pa'i phyir ro zhe na| 'jig rten la grags pa 'am gzhan sel gyi ngor lhan gcig[182] dmigs par btags kyi don la tha dad ma grub pas skyon med do||

[2.3.2.2.3.2.2.2.2.3.3. gtan tshigs 'di ma nges pa spang ba]

gsum pa gtan tshigs 'di ma nges te| gzugs rang snang pa[183] 'am sems dang sems las byung ba 'am sangs rgyas kyi ye shes kyis sems can gyi sems mkhyen pa la stsogs pa[184] lhan gcig[185] dmigs nges zhugs kyang rdzas tha dad <8a> pas so zhe na| de 'ang gzugs dang snang pa[186] ni gzugs dmigs pa snang pa[187] la ltos[188] pa'i srog chags la lhan gcig[189] dmigs pa na rdzas tha dad ma yin te lcags bsregs pa bzhin no|| snang pa[190] la mi ltos pa'i byi la[191] la stsogs[192] pa la lhan gcig[193] dmigs pa med de snang pa[194] med kyang gzugs dang gzugs med kyang snang ba dmigs pa'i phyir lcags dang me tha dad par gnas pa bzhin no|| sems dang sems byung yang rdzas tha dad par mi 'dod do[195]|| sangs rgyas kyi ye shes kyis gzhan gyi sems mkhyen pa ni so so[196] skye bo'i mngon sum gyi dper mi rung ste| rnam 'grel las|

---

179 T1, T2: lta bu'am
180 T1, T2: kyis
181 T1, T2: cig
182 T1, T2: cig
183 T1, T2: ba
184 T1, T2: sogs
185 T1, T2: cig
186 T1, T2: ba
187 T1, T2: ba
188 T1: bltos
189 T1, T2: cig
190 T1, T2: ba
191 T1, T2: ba
192 T1, T2: sogs
193 T1, T2: cig
194 T1, T2: ba
195 T1, T2: de
196 T1, T2: so'i

So there is no fault [here] like the one in the case of the moon in a dream or the appearance of a strand of hair for somebody with vitreus floaters.

[2.3.2.2.3.2.2.2.2.3.2. Rebuttal of contradiction to this reasoning]

[Refutation of] contradiction to this reasoning:[105] "It is because since simultaneity involves the two, [this] argumentation is excluded from [the situation] that there is no different entity." If they say so, then [I, Sa skya Paṇḍita answer:] there is no fault because from the point of worldly opinions and *apoha* in case of concurrent perception the object of imputation is not established as different.

[2.3.2.2.3.2.2.2.2.3.3. Rebuttal of claim that this argumentation is not ascertained]

[Refutation of claim that] this argumentation[106] is not ascertained: "Even though form and appearing or mind and mental acts or primordial consciousness of the Buddha that knows the minds of sentient beings etc., are ascertained by concurrent perception, they are of different substance." If they say so, then [I, Sa skya Paṇḍita answer:] concerning the form and seeing if in the case of the creature that sees appearance of visible form there is concurrent perception, they[107] are not of different substance, like iron and it's hotness. In case of some creature, like a mouse etc. who does not see in the light there is no concurrent perception. It is because even though there is no light, form and what is formless are seen and perceived. It is like iron and fire remaining different. [I, Sa skya Paṇḍita] do not claim that also mind and mental events are of different substance. In the case of knowledge of the minds of others performed by the primordial consciousness of the Buddha the example of perception of individual samsaric being is not proper. It is said in *Pramāṇavārttika*:

gzugs stsogs[197] dang ni sems de ltar||
gzung pa'i[198] mtshid[199] dpyod pa 'di||
ma dag blo can la[200] yin gyi||
rnal 'byor rtogs pa bsam mi khyab[*] ces bya ba dang|

gnas gyur pa'i ye shes bsam gyis mi khyab par rgyud gzhan grub par bshad pa bzhin no|| 'di la bod phal cher sangs rgyas kyi ye shes kyis ma nges pas lhan gcig[201] dmigs nges yang dag gi rtags ma yin no zhes zer ba ni kun du[202] tha snyad pa dang pha rol gzigs pa'i tshad ma'i rnam gzhag mi shes par smra bar zad do||

[2.3.2.2.3.2.2.3. rnam rig la rtsod pa spang ba]
gsum pa rnam rig la rtsod pa spang ba la gsum las

[2.3.2.2.3.2.2.3.1. rig pa'i rtags ma grub pa spang ba]
dang po rig pa'i rtags ma grub pa spang ba ni rig bya rtags su bkod na ma nges| rig byed rtags su bkod na ma grub| de gnyis las gzhan pa'i rig pa tsam mi rnyed do ce[203] na| snga ma gnyis kyis khyad par du ma byas pa'i rig pa tsam 'god de| ba glang[204] gi mtshid[205] dkar zal dang dkar zal ma yin pa'i lkog shal mi 'god kyi lkog shal tsam 'god pa bzhin no||

[2.3.2.2.3.2.2.3.2. rdul phran dang mtshungs pa spang ba]
gnyis pa rdul phran dang mtshungs pa[206] spang ba ni|

sems rgyun yan lag can dang mtshungs||
skad gcig[207] *rdul gyi cha shas bzhin*||
des na skad cig gsum bdag phyir||
gcig dang du ma bral zhes zer|| /25/

[*] PV III 532: rūpādeś cetasaś ca evam aviśuddhadhiyaṃ prati | grāhyalakṣaṇacintā iyam acintyā yogināṃ gatiḥ ||

[197] T1, T2: sogs

[198] T1, T2: ba'i

[199] T1, T2: mtshan nyid

[200] T1, T2: las

[201] T1, T2: cig

[202] T1, T2: tu

[203] T1, T2: zhe

[204] T1, T2: lang

[205] T1, T2: mtshan nyid

[206] T1, T2: mtshungs pa'i rtsod pa

[207] T1, T2: cig

> In case of forms etc. and the mind, this analysis of the characteristics of an [object] apprehended comes from somebody who has an impure mind. Realization of a yogin is inconceivable.[108]

Primordial consciousness as [result] of transformation[109] is inconceivable, as is explained in *Santānāntarasiddhi*.[110] Concerning this in Tibet, the majority said that since it is not ascertained by primordial consciousness of a Buddha, then ascertainment by simultaneous perception is not authentic reasoning. Which means they [actually] said that they do not know the theory of valid cognition that is completely conventional and valid cognition looking at the other side [at the ultimate]. [111]

[2.3.2.2.3.2.2.3. Rebuttal of objections concerning knowledge through the aspect]

Rebuttal of objections concerning knowledge through the aspect has three points and the first one is:

[2.3.2.2.3.2.2.3.1. Rebuttal of [statement that] reasoning proving knowledge is not established]

Rebuttal of [statement that] reasoning proving knowledge is not established is as follows: "If you set up the reason for what is to be known, it is not ascertained. If you set up reason for the knower, it is not established. No other [aspect of] knowledge that is different from this two only will be found." If they say like this, [I, Sa skya Paṇḍita] acknowledge only knowledge that is not made particularly by the two mentioned before. It is like with the definition of the cow that is not asserted by way of dewlap of mixed colors or of one color. To assert just dewlap [is enough].

[2.3.2.2.3.2.2.3.2. Rebuttal of the objection that (act knowledge) is similar to the atom]

Rebuttal of the objection that [act knowledge] is similar to the atom is the following:

> *Continuum of the mind is similar to something that has parts. A moment* [of consciousness] *is like the parts of the atom. Therefore the moment has the nature of the three and that is why it is said to be free from being one and many.* /25/

dbu ma pa rnams na re sems kyang rgyun gcig du[208] <8b> bden na yan lag can 'gog pa'i rigs pa'i 'don pa bsgyur te| gang la dus cha tha dad yod|| de ni gcig du[209] mi rung ngo zhes gsungs pas khegs so|| skad gcig[210] cha med du bden pa yang drug gis gcig[211] car sbyar ba'i rigs pas rdul phran 'jig pa ltar sems kyang| ji ltar skad cig mtha' yod ltar|| thog ma dbus kyang brtag par gyis|| skad cig gsum gyi bdag nyid phyir|| 'jig rten skad cig la mi gnas zhes bya ba'i rigs pas khegs so zhe na| 'di la bod rnams rdul dang skad cig gnyis 'gog pa'i rigs pa mtshungs pas skad cig cha shas can yin no zhes zer ba ni mi tshungs[212] te|

skad cig gsum gyi bdag nyid phyir||
skad cig gcig pa mi srid 'gyur||
skad cig gcig pa mi srid na||
gsum gyi bdag nyid yin pa nyams|| /26/

skad cig ma gcig nyid mi srid de gsum gyi bdag nyid yin pa'i phyir ro|| 'dod na gsum mi srid par thal te rtsom pa'i gcig mi srid pa'i phyir ro|| 'o na rdul phran yang gcig yin na drug yin par 'gal| drug yin na gcig yin pa[213] 'gal bar mtshungs so zhe na| kho bo yang de 'dod pas rdul phran 'jig pa yin no|| 'o na skad cig kyang 'jig go ce[214] na| dus gsum gcig[215] car skye na bden pa zhig na| kho bo cag cig car mi skye ba la skyon ga la yod|

rags pa gcig[216] car bskor pas na||
dbus kyi rdul phran cha bcas 'gyur||
dus gsum cig car mi skye bas||
da lta'i skad cig cha med yin|| /27/

rdul phran dus gcig du[217] ma bskor na rags pa mi rtsom pas bskor ba na dbus kyi rdul cha bcas su 'gyur ro|| dus gsum gcig[218] car skyes na 'das ma 'ongs gnyis kyang da ltar bar thal ba las| 'gags[219] pa dang ma skyes pa dngos por med

[208] T1, T2: tu
[209] T1, T2: tu
[210] T1, T2: cig
[211] T1, T2: cig
[212] T1, T2: mtshungs
[213] T1, T2: par
[214] T1, T2: zhe
[215] T1, T2: cig
[216] T1, T2: cig
[217] T1, T2: tu
[218] T1, T2: cig
[219] T1, T2: 'gag

Madhyamikas say: "If mind is truly one continuum, we will bring forth reasoning refuting that what has parts. Where are the different parts of time? That [what has different parts of time] is not acceptable as the one." Saying so they refute. Also even though the moment [of consciousness] is truly partless, then because of argument of joining the six simultaneously, the particle is destroyed.

> In the same way the mind is similar in that the moment [of it] has boundaries. Taking under consideration beginning and middle, moment is of threefold nature. That is why the world does not abide even for a moment.[112]

With this reasoning they made the refutation. If so, concerning this Tibetans say: "Arguments refuting both atoms and moment are similar, and that is why moment has parts." But they are not similar.

> *Since moment is of threefold nature, one moment will not be possible. If one moment is not possible, being of threefold nature is disintegrated. /26/*

"Moment is not possible as oneness, because it is of threefold nature, it follows that threefold is not possible, because the one from [this] composed [entity] is not possible.[113] Well then, if particle is also one, it contradicts being sixfold. Similarly, if it is sixfold, it contradicts one." If they say so, we also claim that, so particles are destroyed. If they say "moment is also destroyed," then if three times are generated at once, true [existence of the moment] is destroyed. And if it is so, we [say]: what would be the fault in not being generated at once?

> *Since gross* [object] *is surrounded at once, the middle particle would have parts. Since three times are not generated at once, present moment has no parts. /27/*

If the particle is not surrounded at one time, gross [object] is not composed; if it is surrounded, the middle particle would have parts. If three times are generated at once, then it follows that both past and future would be present.[114] So what decayed and what is not generated do not exist as a thing; and out of one moment

pa'i phyir dang| da ltar skyes pa'i skad gcig[220] gcig nyid las dngos po'i chos mi srid pas skad cig la cha shas med pa'i dgongs pa de <9a> yin no|| 'o na rdul phran 'jig pa'i tshe cha bcas su 'jig gam cha med du 'jig ce na| bzhag na cha bcas yin la bshig na cha med du 'jig te[221] skra rtse'i zil pa bzhin no|| kha cig rdul phran thug med du 'dod pa ni dngos po'i de kho na ma shes pa'o|| 'o na skad cig kyang bzhag na cha bcas bshig na cha med du mtshungs pa ma yin nam zhe na| mi tshungs[222] te bzhag kyang skyes tsam gi cha ma gtogs pa cha gzhan med de 'gags pa dang ma skyes pa dngos po[223] med pa'i phyir ro|| des na slob dpon 'phags pa'i skad cig gsum sbrel nas gshigs[224] pa 'dis nyan thos dus gsum rdzas yod du 'dod pa dgag par nus kyi skad cig cha med dgag[225] par mi nus te| 'das ma 'ongs rdzas su ma grub pa'i bar du skad cig gi rdzas gcig bcug kyang dngos po la ma grub la| blos rloms su[226] zin kyang blo'i chos rang dga' bas don mi 'jog[227] ste| ri bong gi rwa gnyis kyi bar du bum pa bcag par rloms[228] kyang mi 'chag[229] pa bzhin no|| 'o na chos kyi grags pas gcig dang du bral gsungs pa dang 'gal lo zhe na| mi 'gal te yul gcig dang du bral lam gzung 'dzin gcig dang du bral la dgongs pa yin no|| kha cig dus gcig dang du bral du gsungs so zhes zer ba ni gzhung gi skabs don ma longs pa yin no|| 'dor na phyogs kyis phye na blo 'ang cha bcas yin la dus kyis phye na yul yang cha med yin no|| des na kun du[230] tha snyad pa'i tshad ma la skad cig cha bcas sam skad cig gtan med du khas blangs na ltos med kyi rtags dang lhan cig mi gnas pa'i 'gal ba'i gnod bya ldog pa'i dus la stsogs[231] pa'i rnam gzhag thams cad 'jig go|| 'o na cha med kyi dngos po srid par 'gyur ro zhe na| skad cig cha med kyi dngos por 'dod pa yin no|| de lta na don dam gyi dngos por 'gyur ro zhe na| spros bral kyi don dam ma yin te 'jig pa'i phyir[232]| don byed nus pa'i don dam yin te <9b> kun du[233] tha snyad pa'i tshad ma dpyod pa'i skabs su

---

[220] T1, T2: cig
[221] T1, T2: ste
[222] T1, T2: mtshungs
[223] T1, T2: por
[224] T1, T2: bshig
[225] T1: 'gag
[226] T1, T2: rlom du
[227] T1, T2: 'jig
[228] T1, T2: rlom
[229] T1, T2: chag
[230] T1, T2: tu
[231] T1, T2: sogs
[232] T1, T2: phyir dang
[233] T1, T2: tu

generated in the presence the phenomenon of the thing is not possible[115] – hence the idea [of Vaibhāṣika] that the moment has no parts.

Well then [Sa skya Paṇḍita answers:], at the time when the particle is destroyed, is something that has parts destroyed or is it destroyed as partless? If [particle] is assumed, it has parts and if it is demolished, it is destroyed as partless.[116] It is like dew drops at the tip of the hair. When somebody claims that particle has no ultimate beginning,[117] he does not know the nature of things.

Well then "If the moment is assumed, then it has parts, so when it is destroyed isn't it similar to a partless one?" If they say so, [Sa skya Paṇḍita answers that] it is not similar because even though it is assumed that, except for only particles that are born, there are no other [particles]. And this is because what decayed and what is not generated do not exist as a thing. Therefore the words of noble master that three moments after being connected are than destroyed, can negate statement of Śrāvakas that the three times are substantial,[118] but cannot negate a partless moment. Because as long as past and future are not established substantially, even though one substance of the moment is set up there, it is not established as a thing. Even though mind exaggerated [that three moments exist], the sole imagination does not destroy the entity. It is like even though one exaggerates trying to crush the vase between two horns of the rabbit, it is not destroyed.[119]

Well then, if they say that this contradicts Dharmakīrti saying that it is free from the one and the many, [I, Sa skya Paṇḍita answer:] there is no contradiction; the idea is that object is free from one and many or the apprehended and the apprehender are free from one and many. The one who said that time is free from the one and the many, didn't get the meaning of the text. Shortly speaking, if you analyze in terms of sides, mind also has parts. If you analyze in terms of time, object also is partless. Therefore, if to claim that in completely conventional valid cognition moment has parts or moment does not exist at all, then all explanations like the one at the time of refuting what is to be invalidated with "the reason of no relation"[120] and contradiction of not abiding together are destroyed.[121]

Well then, if they say that a partless thing is possible, [I, Sa skya Paṇḍita] claim the moment that is partless thing. If they say, well that being so, this is the absolute thing, [I, Sa skya Paṇḍita answer that] it is not the absolute free from elaborations,[122] because it [can be] destroyed. It is the absolute that is effective, because when analyzed in terms of completely conventional valid cognition, all that is

'khrul ba[234] dang ma 'khrul ba[235] thams cad skad cig la rag las pa'i phyir[236]|| chos thams cad bdag med pa'i rten yang de yin te| rnam 'grel las|

> nged kyi de 'ang[237] rkyen las skyes||
> de ni[238] bdag med lta rten yin[*] zhes gsungs pas so||

gnas gyur pa'i ye shes thob nas skad cig gis 'jig pa la stsogs[239] pa thams cad gnas gyur pa'i phyir rnam pa thams cad du bsam gyis mi khyab po zhes bshad zin to||

[2.3.2.2.3.2.2.3.3. rnam pa yong med la brtags na mi 'thad pa spang pa]
gsum pa rnam pa yod med la brtags na mi 'thad pa spang pa ni shes pa rnam bcas rnam med gang yin yang rung ste bden brdzun mtshungs pa la tshad ma dang tshad ma ma yin pa'i rnam gshag 'gal lo ce[240] na|

> *don du snang ba blo nyid yin||*
> *snang ba de nyid phyi na med||*
> *bag chags brtan dang mi brtan la||*
> *bden dang brdzun[241] pa'i rnam gzhag byed||* /28/

snang ba ci skyes pa shes pa yin la| de 'ang phyi rol gyi yul du grub pa med cing| yul med par mtshungs kyang bag chags brtan pa'i sgo nas zla ba gcig dang dung dkar po la stsogs[242] pa tshad mar 'jog la| zla ba gnyis dang dung ser po la stsogs[243] pa bag chags mi brtan pa'i phyir tshad ma ma yin par 'jog go|| gzhan grub mtha'i dbye ba kho pos[244] byas pa'i grub mtha' rnam 'byed la stsogs[245] par shes par bya bas 'dir ma spros so||

---

[*] PV II 253ab: sā ca naḥ pratyayotpattiḥ sā nairātmyadgāśrayaḥ |
[234] T1, T2: pa
[235] T1, T2: pa
[236] T1, T2: phyir ro
[237] T1, T2: yang
[238] T1, T2: yang
[239] T1, T2: sogs
[240] T1, T2: zhe
[241] T1: rdzun
[242] T1, T2: dung dkar 'dzin la sogs
[243] T1, T2: dung ser 'dzin la sogs
[244] T1, T2: bos
[245] T1, T2: sogs

erroneous and non-erroneous is dependent on the moment [of mind]. It [moment] is also the basis of selflessness of all phenomena, since *Pramāṇavārttika* says:

> We ourselves are also born from conditions. And they are also the basis for the view of selflessness.[123]

It has been explained that having attained transformed primordial consciousness, everything like [mind] destroyed momentarily etc. is transformed, and that is why it is inconceivable in all aspects.

[2.3.2.2.3.2.2.3.3. Rebuttal (of argumentation that) if aspects are examined whether they exist or not, they are not acceptable]

Rebuttal [of argumentation that] if aspects are examined whether they exist or not, they are not acceptable is the following: Whatever cognition having aspects or not having aspects[124] is fine – they are similar [both having] true and false [aspect]. So presentation of [the first one as] valid cognition and [the second as] not valid cognition is contradictory, they say [and Sa skya Paṇḍita answers:]

> *Appearances of entities are mind itself. These appearances are not outside. Through stable and unstable karmic tendencies they are presented as true and false.* /28/

Whatever appearance is generated, it is cognition. And also even though outer objects are not established and are similar to nonexistent object, by way of stable karmic tendencies the apprehending of one moon and white conch etc. is posited as valid cognition. The apprehending of two moons and yellow conch etc. because of unstable mental tendencies is posited as not being valid cognition. Division of other tenet systems should be known from my *Grub mtha' rnam 'byed* etc., so I didn't elaborate on them here. To cut a long story short:

ji srid phyi rol khas len pa||
de srid rgyu la gzung yul zer||
shes bya nang gir zhugs pa na||
yul dang yul can grub pa med|| /29/

bsdu ba'i tshigs su bcad pa'o||

rigs pa'i gter[246] las yul brtag pa'i rab tu byed pa dang po'o||

[246] T1, T2: tshad ma rigs pa'i gter

> *As long as the outer is accepted, for that long the cause is said to be an apprehended object. If what is to be cognized is posited as inside one, object and subject are not established.* /29/

So is the "Object Analysis" being the first chapter of *Treasury of Epistemology*.

Notes

[1] The role of object universal [*don spyi*] cf. Dreyfus (1997: 251–260); Stoltz (2006); Tillemans (1999: 163–164, 220–222). Also cf. footnote 5 below.

[2] In original *med snang*, which is the abbreviation of *med pa gsal snang*. For an analysis of its status in this context cf. Introduction.

[3] Sa skya Paṇḍita challenges here the realist view of Phya pa and his followers. The main difference at issue here between realists and anti-realists is well summarized by Dreyfus (with different terminology): "The first key epistemological move made by the realists is to break the isolation of thought by reinterpreting the concept of the object of thought. This rein-terpretation concerns two types of object, the appearing object (*snang yul*) or its equivalent, the held object (*gzung yul*), and the object of application (*'jug yul*). These concepts, which can be traced back to Dharmottara, have been stressed by Tibetan epistemologists as part of an elaborate typology of object, which we will examine later, first proposed by Cha-ba. They are meant to account for and underline the cognitive aspect of cognition, the fact that consciousness reveals objects.

For Cha-ba and his followers, this explanation plays a particularly important role in their epistemology, for it provides a way to strengthen the connection between thought and reality. Thus, the intentional interpretation of the object of application examined earlier and the explanations of the concept of appearing object that follow are intended as realist explanations of how thought apprehends reality. According to this account, the conception of my rocking chair, for example, is not strictly enclosed in the realm of concepts, as antirealists maintain. Although this conception primarily apprehends the object universal of chair, it also applies to a real chair. Antirealists agree with this last statement but understand it in pragmatic terms. My thought of a chair applies practically to a real chair. By contrast, Cha-ba understands application in intentional terms. That is, the thought of a chair applies to the real chair in that it apprehends it. In this way, Cha-ba and his disciples offer a realist explanation of the relation between thought and reality. Instead of being limited to unreal constructs, thought is said to apprehend reality itself through the mediation of constructs." Dreyfus (1997: 322).

[4] Cf. definition of appearing object in *Tshad ma rigs gter* in Go rams pa's commentary.

[5] Dreyfus comments this realistic approach as follows: "The appearing object of a conception (*rtog pa'i snang yul*), understood in a technical sense, is necessarily unreal. It must be distinguished from the real object that appears to that conception (*yul de rtog pa la snang ba*). Accordingly, ajar, for example, appears to a conceptual cognition but is not its appearing object, which is the object universal of the jar. This artificial distinction is made to conciliate the Ge-luk view of thought and language as partially reflecting reality with Dharmakīrti's assertion that thought does not take real things as its objects of comprehension (*meya*, *gzhal bya*). According to this interpretation, Dharmakīrti did not intend to exclude that real things appear to thought but only that they are their appearing objects in the technical sense of the word. Only object universals are the appearing objects of conceptual thought. Real entities are not appearing objects of thought even though they appear to it." Dreyfus (1997: 323).

[6] Generally speaking, Sa skya Paṇḍita does not agree with the position of his adversaries that erroneous cognition has to have an object. He rather tends to claim that it is erroneous just because of not grasping an object. As Stoltz comment on this fragment: "As we can see from this quoted

passage, Sa-pan and his philosophical interlocutors are at odds about what ontological commitments are required in order to maintain the view that certain cognitions are unsound. Sa-pan's position is that formulating the relevant points concerning cognition can be made without committing one to 'tagalong' existential claims, whereas his opponents are presented as maintaining the view that a coherent position about the soundness of cognitions can only be upheld if we antecedently grant that the appearing entities in all cognitions exist as epistemically evaluable objects of thought.

In looking at the passage cited above, it is evident that much of the argumentative interplay between Sa-pan and his philosophical interlocutors with respect to the status of concepts hinges on the notion of an unsound cognition (*'khrul shes*). In my elucidation of Sa-pan's first argument it will become quite clear that part of what is at issue in these historical Tibetan debates is just how we are to interpret the notion of 'unsoundness.' Obviously, speaking of the soundness, or lack thereof, of a cognition is rather remote from contemporary analytic philosophy. My intent in representing the relevant Tibetan term with this locution is to communicate the idea that there is something defective about unsound cognitions, and yet these cognitions are still held to be capable of providing knowledge. Within this domain of philosophical discourse, Tibetans are in agreement that the unsoundness of any cognition concerns an error with respect to the phenomenal entity (*snang yul*) of that cognition. What is in dispute between Sa-pan and his Kadampa interlocutors is just what it is about these phenomenal entities that renders their corresponding cognitions un- sound, even though these cognitions might still bestow knowledge." Stoltz (2006: 570).

[7] Subschool of Sthaviravāda. Concerning the view of Sthavira on that topic cf. Dhammajoti (2007: 121–122, 163–164, 168, n. 8).

[8] Generally speaking, sound universal [*sgra spyi, śabdasāmānya*] is mental representation of the spoken word associated with the object universal [*don spyi, arthasāmānya*]. For an analysis of this pair of terms cf. Pind (1991). Cf. also Introduction. A very similar idea can be found in de Saussure's writing about so called sound-images and concepts: "mental facts (concepts) are associated with representations of the linguistic sounds (sound-images) that are used for their expression. A given concept unlocks a corresponding sound-image in the brain; this purely psychological phenomenon is followed in turn by a physiological process: the brain transmits an impulse corresponding to the image to the organs used in producing sounds. [...] from the ear to the brain, the physiological transmission of the sound-image; in the brain, the psychological association of the image with the corresponding concept." de Saussure (1966: 11–12). Concerning the comparison of theories of language in Sa skya Paṇḍita and de Saussure cf. Ottmer (2003).

[9] Mental acts [*caitasika, sems las byung ba*] are classified as so-called accompanying mind [*khor sems*] whose function is to grasp individual characteristics of any cognized object. They accompany the so called main mind [*gtso sems*] that grasps the object in its essence.

[10] The so-called non-associated factor [*viprayukta saṃskāra, ldan pa ma yin pa'i 'dus byed*] or the factor which is not associated with mind – together with factors associated with mind – belongs to the fourth skandha. Traditionally non-associated factor is divided into 13, 14 or 24 types.

[11] Cf. comments on this fragment in Hugon (2008: 152–156).

[12] For detailed analysis of this argument cf. Stoltz (2006: 571–574).

[13] As Stoltz summarizes the view Sa skya Paṇḍita opposes: "According to Sa-pan, they maintained that for each and every cognition there must be a corresponding robustly existing phenomenal entity. In acts of sensory cognition the cognitive episodes take as their phenomenal objects real objects (in successful acts of perception) or illusions (in unsuccessful cognitive acts). In conceptual cognition mental episodes map to a concept. Sa-pan, by contrast, forcefully asserts that a restriction must be placed on the class of cognitions for which there correspond robustly existing phenomenal entities. His view is that a robustly existing entity only appears to the mind in those cases in which the cognition is itself sound. For any cognition that is unsound, although we may say in a loose sense that there is still something appearing to the agent's mind, Sa-pan denies that this item exists as an entity that can be epistemically judged. As an illustration, let us suppose that a person has an awareness as of a chair being in her field of vision. Sa-pan's view is that acknowledging the

robust existence of a chair demands that this person's perception was not in some way faulty. In an unsound perceptual act, the illusion that appears to a perceiver is held not to exist robustly – which is to say that what appears is not something about which informed epistemic claims can be made." Stoltz (2006: 571).

[14] What is meant here is the visual phenomenon caused by eye illness called vitreus floaters [*muscae volintantes*] when the patient has an impression of seeing small strand of hairs. The example used very often in Buddhist epistemology.

[15] Reference to famous example from *Hastavālanāmprakaraṇa*. Cf. Tola, Dragonetti (1995: 1–17). The discussion of the use of this example in Sa skya Paṇḍita cf. Stoltz (2006: 573–574).

[16] For detailed analysis of this argument that can be called "the argument from manifestation" cf. Stoltz (2006: 574–578).

[17] PV III 376ab.

[18] As Stoltz points out, the line of reasoning here is very much in tune with post-Wittgensteinian approach: "As one can see, Sa-pan is speaking of these entities as though they would be private objects – constituents of the private states of a single person, unknowable by others. Insofar as he speaks about private objects being unknowable by others, it seems that Sa-pan is arguing for the *epistemic* privacy of such entities (were they to exist). That is, concepts would be *in principle* unknowable by others, as opposed to merely unknown. This is an interesting thought, first of all because it is quite similar to arguments about private states and private languages in our own analytic tradition, but also because Sa-pan's comments were developed during the first half of the thirteenth century. Much like the arguments used by post-Wittgensteinian thinkers, Sa-pan seeks to prove that there cannot be such things as private objects. There are two types of arguments that are commonly made when arguing about private objects and the difficulties of gaining knowledge of them: arguments from *acquisition* and arguments from *manifestation*. Arguments from acquisition purport to show that one person could never acquire, in her own mind, the private objects of another person, whereas arguments from manifestation claim that even if she does happen to acquire the private objects of another person, she could never be in a position to realize that the right object has arisen in her mind." Stoltz (2006: 576).

[19] PV III 376cd.

[20] This is the argument identified by Stoltz as an argument from acquisition: "This is an instance of the so-called *argument from acquisition*. Understanding – which is to say, knowledge – of another person's private concepts is in principle impossible because there is no means by which to examine the (private) object about which another person is speaking. This inability to compare one another's concepts calls into doubt our ability to hit upon the right concept when attempting to engage in communication with other persons; and this inability is sufficient grounds for denying that one can gain knowledge of the phenomenal entities arising in another's conceptual thought." Stoltz (2006: 576).

[21] More precisely, if one is able to relate to the object in one's own mind and in the mind of somebody to whom that object is explained, and also the one to whom was explained can relate to the object in the mind of the explainer, the object is in fact one and the same.

[22] PV III 337.

[23] Cf. Go rams pa's remark on the meaning of *spyi* in his commentary translated below.

[24] This is, according to Stoltz, the argument from manifrstation: "Sa-pan offers the following dilemma: Let us grant that conventions of language are used to identify (believed) similarities between peoples' phenomenal states. Now, in any given instance in which one person A employs such a convention, the correct phenomenal entity either does or does not appear to person B. Let us suppose that the concept about which person A is speaking does in fact dawn in person B's mind. Here, the conceptual appearance that dawns in person B's mind is person B's private object, and not numerically identical to whatever conceptual appearance arises in person A's mind. Therefore, person B is still not in a position to realize that the concepts actually do match up correctly. If, on the other hand, the correct concept does not arise in person B's mind, then she is similarly in no position to recognize a mutual similarity between A's object and her own object. In either case, this

inability to *realize* that one has hit upon the correct concept in those cases when the right concept does dawn in one's mind again threatens our claims to knowledge of another's private concepts. This is an instance of the *argument from manifestation*." Stoltz (2006: 577).

[25] PV III 378.

[26] What is meant here is the fact that space is not an object – like a tree, for example – to be seen. So even when one is looking into the sky one is not seeing it; one does not see an object. That is why the one who claims to see it is a fool.

[27] For discussion on the perceptible in *Tshad ma rigs gter* cf. Introduction.

[28] The discussion of this statement cf. Yoshimizu (2004), Hugon (2011).

[29] In original *don byed nus pa* (*arthakriyāsamartham*) translated usually as "able to perform a function." More on *arthakriyā* cf. Dunne (2004: 256–259). In this context particularily cf. Hugon (2011).

[30] PV III 53d–54ab.

[31] PV III 64cd.

[32] For definition of the apprehended object in *Tshad ma rigs gter* according to Go rams pa ini his commentary below.

[33] For definition of the indirect [*lkog gyur*] in *Tshad ma rigs gter* cf. Go rams pa's commentary. There are the two terms used by Sa skya Paṇḍita – *lkog gyur* and *lkog na mo*. More cf. Dreyfus (1997: 416–427).

[34] For definition of the conceived object in *Tshad ma rigs gter* according to Go rams pa cf. in his commentary translated below.

[35] Sa skya Paṇḍita refers here to the objection to his claim that there is only one object of cognition, which is supposed to contradict Dignāga claiming that there are two. More on object of cognition in Dignāga cf. Chu (2006).

[36] Discussion of this objection cf. Hugon (2008: 159–160).

[37] PV III 54cd.

[38] PV III 1ab.

[39] As Gold sums up the approach od Sa skya Paṇḍita: "For Sa-Paṇ, perceptions do not have erroneous objects; if they are erroneous, *they have no object*. The same, then, is true of all conceptual constructions: they are not conceptually shaped mental 'objects' appearing to inferential cognitions; *they simply do not exist*. In both cases, the philosopher's mistake is in positing some kind of quasi-existence for things that appear. But when we remember the Sautrāntika notion that causality is the touchstone of the real, it is easy to dismiss the possibility that what is only an appearance may be a real thing. What causes erroneous appearances is the defective perceptual apparatus itself, not some erroneous object." Gold (2014: 362).

[40] PV III 1cd.

[41] PV III 7ab.

[42] PV III 8–9ab.

[43] This argument is based on Sa skya Paṇḍita's claim – mentioned already – that cognition which is not valid is the one that does have any object. That is why valid cognition invalidates the idea of grasping non-existent objects. Cf. note 13 and 39.

[44] PV III 16bc.

[45] The conclusion meant here by Dharmakīrti is that in that case the universal would turn out to be a particular.

[46] PV III 9c–10a.

[47] By the result Dharmakīrti refers here to the outcome of valid cognition that is based on the object to which the cognitive process refers. In this case the object can be nonexistent as well. More on that topic cf. Hugon (2011) who summarizes that poin as follows: "what does not exist, whether an absence or a non-entity, provided it becomes the target of human interest »under some circumstances,« can be conceptualized (in the form of a universal), and such a concept can be manipulated just like any other, and can also lead to an inquiry about its having or not having some grounding in reality (*bhāvopadāna*)." Hugon (2011: 378).

[48] Dharmakīrti means here that the androgynous as a person of undecided sex cannot be the object of sexual lust, so there is no sense in deciding whether the androgynous is beautiful or not.

[49] PV I 210–211.

[50] Glo bo mkhan chen in his commemntary [L 21] takes it as a reference cittamātra view in Dharmakīrti and Vasubandhu, namely to PV III 360 (cf. note 91 below) and to *Viṃśatikā* 12: "If six [atoms] were joined at once to one atom, it would have six parts. And if six were in one place, this mass would be one atom only [*ṣaṭkena yugapadayogāt paramāṇoḥ ṣaḍaṃśarā/ ṣaṇṇāṃ samānadeśatvāt piṇḍaḥ syād aṇumātrakaḥ*]."

[51] Since self-knowledge does not have an object.

[52] Meaning Buddhist and non-Buddhist ones.

[53] Īśvara.

[54] *Pradhan* – epithet of Viṣṇu.

[55] Here *rnam rig* is synonymous with *sems tsam pa* – Cittamātra.

[56] The theory of nature as first cause cf. Bhattacharya (2012).

[57] The so called "leftovers eaters [*gzegs zan pa*]" are the followers of Kaṇāda (Kaṇabhakṣa or Kaṇabhuj, around 200–400 A.D.), legendary founder of Vaiśeṣika whose names mean "atom eater."

[58] The view of Svātantrika Madhyamaka.

[59] The view of Prāsangika Madhyamaka.

[60] As Sa skya Paṇḍita sums up, what all above mentioned views have in common is the duality of subject and object (which can be of course differently interpreted, and finally is shown by Madhyamikas to be nonexistent on the absolute level).

[61] For the refutation of this view cf. *Madhyamakāvatāra* VI 99–100: "If the things are created completely without any cause, then everything would be permanently created from everything; and also worldly people would not collect the crops by hundreds of ways to make it appear like planting the seeds etc. If samsaric beings were devoid of cause, they would be ungraspable like scent and colour of utpala flower. So since we do perceive the world in its great variety, understand that the world, like your own mind, comes from a cause [*gal te rgyu med kho nar skye bar lta shig 'gyur na ni| |de tshe mtha' dag rtag tu thams cad las kyang skye 'gyur zhing| |'bras 'byung ched du 'jig rten 'di yi sa bon la sogs ni| |brgya phrag dag gi sgo nas sdud par byed par yang mi 'gyur|| gal te 'gro ba rgyu yis stong par gyur na nam mkha' yi| |utpa la yi dri mdog ji bzhin gzung du med nyid na| |shin tu ches bkra'i 'jig rten 'dzin pa'ang yin pa de yi phyir| |rang gi blo bzhin 'jig rten rgyu las yin par shes par gyis||*]."

[62] PV I 35ab.

[63] The argument is based on the classical *pramāṇa* axiom that what is permanent is not effective, and thus it can not act; and particularly in this case it is not effective as a creator.

[64] PV III 219.

[65] Knowledge of the entity [*don rig*] refers generally to Hīnayāna schools maintaining the existence of outer objects and knowledge through the aspect [*rnam rig*] refers to the Mind Only School.

[66] The word *chod pa* literally means that which is cut off in the sense that it is not directly accessible. It is used as a synonym of *lkog gyur* so it is translated here with the same word.

[67] Sa skya Paṇḍita refers here to the division of faculties into two: faculty with support [*rten bcas kyi dbang po*] and the faculty similar to it [*de mtshungs kyi dbang po*]. The first one is responsible for perception during the waking state when there is a contact with real object, the other is active in the state of sleep (For more on them in the context of Buddhist epistemology cf. Perdue (1992: 218n.). Generally, according to Vaibhāṣika view the object, the faculty and the consciousness have to be simultaneous, otherwise perception would be impossible. If the object and faculty preceded the consciousness, it would come about without any basis since at the time of its arisal the object and faculty are gone. This would also mean that sensory consciousness has past object which is impossible. Cf. Dhammajoti (2007: 139–141).

[68] According to Vaibhāṣika, the object is perceived directly by sensory consciousness that is simultaneous with the object and sense faculty. The process of seeing, for example, is based on the

physical organ – the eye – made of substance that has the nature of seeing (which is later questioned by Sa skya Paṇḍita). Thre process of perception, according to Vaibhāṣika, takes place when three aspects are simulataneously present: the object, the eye and the consciousness of seeing whis is their simultaneous effect. More on Vaibhāṣika model of perception cf. Dhammajoti (2007: 136–144).

[69] Two possible relations are meant here: relation of the same nature (*ngo bo bdag cig gi 'brel ba*) and relation of the one arising from the other (*de 'byung gi 'brel ba*). They both are impossible since the object and subject can not be of the same essence like for example fire and hotness and they can not arise from each other because this would mean that one is prior to the other which contradicts their simultaniety.

[70] Namely, they reject Vaibhāṣika view as indicated in the previous passage.

[71] As it is explained below, the consciousness has to have the cause to arise and this should be the thing to be perceived. According to madhyamaka simultaneously appearing entities cannot be in causal relationship because exactely due to their simultaneity it is impossible to determine which one is the cause and which one is the effect that should follow the cause. If the object and consciousness appeared simultaneously, the consciousness would actulally arise without the cause (which is the sense coming into contact with the object).

[72] In original *yid la byed pa* which is the translation of sanskrit *manasikāra*. One of 51 mental acts (*caitasika, sems byung*) that belong to the group of the five omnipresent mental states (*sarvatraga, kun tu 'gro lnga*).

[73] The mountain in South India.

[74] Sa skya Paṇḍita claims that there is no need of simultaneous object with consciousness in the following way: in the first moment there are three factors simultaneous: object, sens faculty and mental focusing. In the second moment consciousness is generated. And now if this consciousness needs simultaneous object there should be the second object in the second moment to be experienced by the cosciousness. This however would require also second faculty etc.

[75] PV III 224ab.

[76] PVin I 15. Cf. Vetter (1966: 57). What is meant here is the fact that by way of concomitance if there is the object, the consciousness appears and by reverse concomitance the fact that if there is not any object there is no consciousness.

[77] Unidentified sutra.

[78] Meaning: first the similitude of the aspect of outer object arises in the mind, and afterwards it is perceived by consciousness which is similar (takes the form of) to that generated similitude.

[79] These two mean: 1) collection of object, sense faculty and focusing and 2) cognition caused by them.

[80] Detailed explanation of Sautrāntika model of perception cf. Dhammajoti (2007: 158–162).

[81] PV III 369.

[82] For example in case of the rice sprout, the main cause is rice seed. Water etc. are secondary causes or conditions.

[83] PV III 371d.

[84] It refers to the argument that the situation when some hidden invisible object posits the aspect is in fact similar to the situation when the aspect would be posited by an invisible ghost.

[85] This quotation from Dharmakīrti is not listed in *Verse-Index of Dharmakīrti's works (Tibetan versions)* by E. Steinkellner. Tibetan Classics edition of Go rams pa's commentary where it is also cited does not identify the source of quotation but only indicates that this sentence is similar to Sa skya Paṇḍita's formulation from his autocommentary. In *dbu ma rgyan gyi rnam bshad 'jam dbyangs bla ma dgyes pa'i zhal lung* by *'jam mgon 'ju mi pham rnam rgyal rgya mtsho* (*The Complete Explanation of* Madhyamakālaṃkāra *Called Oral Transmission Rejoicing the Guru Manjuśri*) which is his commentary to Śāntarakṣita's *Madhyamakālaṃkāra*, this sentence is quoted again and attributed again explicitly to Dharmakīrti. All editions of Go rams pa's commentary I used render this sentence as follows: *gal te phy rol dpyod la 'jug pa ni/ kho bos mdo sde'i skabs la rnam par brten/* while Jamgön Mipham version reads: *gal te phy rol dpyod la 'jug pa ni/ kho bo mdo sde'i skas*

la rnam par brten/. Apart from small difference in case of agentive particle, there is also *skas* instead of *skabs* in the version from 'jam mgon mi pham. In translation I follow his version, since *skabs* does not make good sense in the sentence.

[86] The reasoning is an analysis of the question whether two atoms connected together become bigger than one atom or not. If the answer is yes, it means they have parts which contradicts its partlesness. If the answer is they do not grow bigger, it means one can not create the heap because two, there, thousand of atoms together are not different in size.

[87] The house which obviously has parts because of having sides.

[88] Here subtle atom (*phra rab rdul*) as indivisible atom is differentiated from particle (*rdul phran*) composed of seven former ones.

[89] *Viṃśatikā* 12.

[90] The reasoning similar to the one explained above (note 86). It is an analysis whether attaching another atom to the atom that is partless makes it longer or not. If the answer is that they do not change the size it is impossible to differentiate small collection from big collection and impossible to build the house collecting atoms. If the answer is that they change size it means they have to have parts which contradicts their partlessness.

[91] PV III 360cd or PVin I 51cd.

[92] On the opponents of Sa skya Paṇḍita cf. Hugon (2012).

[93] Here Sa skya Paṇḍita assumes the division of worldly beings explained for example in *Bodhicaryāvatāra*. Worldly beings (*'jig rten pa*) there are divided into ordinary ones (*phal pa*) and yogic ones (*rnal 'byor*). The latter are divided into non-Buddhist ones (*phyi rol pa*) and Buddhists (*nang pa*). The latter into Vaibhāṣika (*bye brag smra ba*) and Sautrāntika (*mdo sde pa*).

[94] Go rams pa in his commentary defines it also as "clear and experiencing [*gsal zhing myong ba*]." G 50. The definition of mind as knowing (*rig pa*) in Sa skya Paṇḍita cf. Przybyslawski (2016: 393–395).

[95] Example illustrating that the essential quality cannot be separated from what is established by it. In this case the cow by definition is established by dewlap.

[96] The exact inference Sa skya Paṇḍita refers to is presented in the commentary to Śāntarakṣita's *Madhyamakālaṃkāra* by 'jam mgon mi pham rgya mtsho: "The main one that proves that object and subject are not different is the inference showing that all appearances are created by nature of consciousness that is clear and knowing; and [the inference] proving with concurrent seeing that is certain. Here it is seen by valid cognition that the object which is blue color and consciousness grasping the blue are both concurrent. It is sure and certain that it is not contingent [situation]. Here the following inference is put: The possessor of property is an object that is blue color and the mind grasping the blue; they are not of different substance, because certainly they are always seen together. Like seeing two moons. If somebody wonders why they must be of one nature if certainly they are seen concurrently?, [the answer is:] if something is not of the one substance, it must be of different substance. This reason [that they are certainly see together] is impossible as put for something that is of different substance; like for example the colors blue and golden etc. [they are different so can be seen separately] [*gzung 'dzin rdzas thad dad ma yin par sgrub pa'i gsto bo snang ba thams cad shes pa gsal rig gi ngo bor skyes pa'i gtan tshigs dang/ lhan cig dmigs nges kyis sgrub par byed pa yin te/ de la yul sngon po dang sngo 'dzin gyi shes pa gnyis dus lhan cig tu tshad mas dmigs pa dang/ de'ng res 'ga' ba ma yin par gtan du khyab pa'm nges pa ste 'di ltar/ yul sngon po dang sngo 'dzin gyi blo chos can/ rdzas gzhan ma yin te/ lhan cig dmigs pa nges pa'i phyir/ zla gnyis snang bzhin/ zhes 'god pa'o// de la lhan cig dmigs par nges na ci'i phyir rdzas gcig yin dgos so snyam na/ gang rdzas gcig ma yin na rdzas tha dad yin dgos la/ rdzas tha dad la rtags de zhugs pa mi srid de sngo ser la sogs pa bzhin no/*]." M 183.

[97] The inference called "the inference of perceiving what is pervaded being contradictory to the pervader [*khyab byed dang 'gal ba'i khyab bya dmigs pa*]" as presented in the footnote above is meant here to say that what is pervaded is the fact of not being of the different substance and the pervader is certainty that they are seen concurrently.

[98] PVin I 55b. The original form of this argumentation referring to the blue color and two moons cf. Vetter (1966: 95–97).

[99] On *trairūpya* in Sa skya Paṇḍita cf. Tillemans (2004) and Hugon (2004).

[100] Namely, the subject of this reasoning is: the blue and the consciousness apphehending blue. They are not different substances, because they are perceived concurrently (according to cittamātra concurrent perception is self-knowlegdge).

[101] Pervasion here establishes that in case of concurrent perception there is no outer object different from the mind. Literally, according to classical *trairūpya* model, it is formulated as follows: if they are not different substances, they are pervaded by concurrent perception. Like in the example of two moons.

[102] *gnod pa can gyi rtags* is the type of correct reason referring to invalid reasoning being rejected by it. In *Tshad ma rigs gter* Sa skya Paṇḍita himself does not give any definition of this type of reason but uses it in chapter six, where he provides such examples. In particular, he rejects Hindu philosophers claiming that even though Iśvara is created/born, he is permanent, which is of course not true in the light of Buddhist philosophy: "If that which is permanent is not effective, it is in tune with [Buddhist] understanding, because it is not a thing. If this effective [object] changes it is not permanent; if there is no change in it, it contradicts activity [*rtag des don byed mi nus na// dngos med yin phyir don la mthun// nus de 'gyur na rtag pa nyams// 'gyur ba med na byed pa 'gal//*]." TR 176. The *gnod pa can gyi rtags* is used to show that making this kind of exception for certain objects is basically wrong, because of contradicting the general definition under which the object is subsumed, which comes down to claiming the same quality is present in the object under discussion and *sapakṣa*. Technically speaking it is in this case the argumentation – as Go rams pa says – "showing the mistake of common ground in case of a thing [which by definition is impermanent] and permanence being *sapakṣa* [*dngos po dang/ mi mthun phyogs rtag pa'i gzhi mthun la gnod pa ston pa'o*]." G 95.

[103] Repetition of the argument from the discussion above.

[104] Kalyāṇa Rākṣasa – Indian exponent of Sautrāntika.

[105] Namely reasoning saying that in case of concurrent perception there is no object different from the mind.

[106] As in the above footnote.

[107] The consciousness of that living being and the object perceived.

[108] PV III 532.

[109] What is meant here is the fact that every wisdom is the transformation of sentient being's ordinary mind.

[110] Reference to the last verse of this Dharmakīrti's text saying: "It is inconceivable how Bhagavān embrace all entities with his mind [*bcom ldan 'das kyis don thams cad thugs su chud pa ni bsam gyis mi khyab ste/*]," *rgyud gzhan grub pa zhes bya ba'i rab tu byed pa* in: *tshad ma rigs pa'i skor rgya gzhung rtsa 'grel bdam bsgrigs: deb dang po. rdo rje rgyal pos bdam bsgrigs byas pa*, Beijing: mi rigs dpe skrun khang, 1988, Vol. 1: 583.

[111] The argument meant here is the following: "In case of the color blue, it is not a different substance from eye consciousness grasping the blue color, because it is ascertained by concurrent perception." And in case of primordial consciousness this kind of reasoning is not true since it can perceive the mind of other beings, which is different from primordial consciousness itself. So the opinion of the majority of Tibetan scholars is not right according to Sa Pan, and Tibetan scholars saying so prove in fact their lack on knowledge about different types of valid cognition.

[112] Kamalaśīla 227b.

[113] Every moment has its beginning, middle and end making the sequence of past, past present and future. If it is supposed that every moment is of this threefold natue, also even one part of it is not possible because again it has beginning middle and end etc.

[114] If the past present and future are created at one it means that past and future are simultaneous with presence and thsu should be preset.

[115] Meaning no object can come about because it requires the proces of generation pressuposing past, present and future.

[116] It is destroyed as partless because after destruction of atom there are no parts left.

[117] What is meant here is the view that atoms can be infinitely divided without obtaining the final indivisible particle.

[118] Reference to the view of Vaibhāṣika that there are three particular substances of time.

[119] Three times are interdependent so any position claiming that one of them is established is contradictory. If the present is established then by way of interdependence past and future is established as well etc. And if past and future are not established you cannot establish the present that depends on them, because nonexistent objects cannot do anything, just like the two horns of the rabbit (one being past and the other the future) cannot crush the vase.

[120] Reason of no relation [*ltos med kyi rtags*] refers to self-sufficiency of the quality discussed which can be explained only by the nature of the object without relating to any external cause. It is not defined in *Tshad ma rigs gter* but in chapter six is used explicitly: "The very [object] which is created is what is being destroyed. In this case there is no need of other destroying factor [*skyes pa kho na 'jig pa yin// de la 'jig byed gzhan mi dgos//*]." T1 167.

[121] For more on this type of contradiction in Buddhist epistemology cf. Rogers (2009: 242–256).

[122] There are two types of the absolute: the absolute that is free from elaborations, which is absolute truth, and the absolute that can perform the function (on relative level).

[123] PV II 253ab.

[124] More on the role of aspect in Buddhist epistemology cf. Kellner (2014); McClintock (2014); Moriyama (2014); Dhammajoti (2007: 171–185).

EDITION AND TRANSLATION OF THE FIRST CHAPTER OF *TSHAD MA RIGS PA'I GTER GYI DON GSAL BAR BYED PA*

<1b/386>

nam mkha' khyab par gar stabs sgyur ba'i sku ni nyi ma 'char ka'i dkyil ltar mdzes||
nam mkha'i mtha' klas sgra chen sgrogs pa'i gsung ni yi ge drug pa rdo rje'i sgra||
nam mkha'i lam la rab tu gnas pa'i thugs ni shes rab ye shes me bo[1] che||
nam mkha'i mtha' la longs spyod mdzad la 'dud do ye shes snang ba lam me[2] stsol||

rigs pa'i gtsug rgyan phyogs glang grags pa'i gzhung||
rigs pa mkhyen pas ji bzhin phye ba'i srol||
rigs pa'i gter gyi kha 'byed legs bshad 'di||
rigs pa don gnyer skal ldan rnams la sbyin||

sde bdun mdo dang bcas pa'i dgongs pa phyin ci ma log par 'grel pa tshad ma rigs pa'i gter gyi don gsal bar bshad pa 'di la gnyis te| shes bya spyi <2a/387> ldog gnas gtan la dbab pa dang| shes byed tshad ma'i rang bzhin nges par bya ba'o| |dang po la gsum ste| shes bya'i yul| shes byed kyi blo| blo des yul rtogs pa'i tshul lo||

---

[1] K1: po
[2] K2: mer

Opening verses of *Tshad ma rigs pa'i gter gyi don gsal bar byed pa*

The *kāya* pervading space in a dance-like manner is beautiful like the disc of rising Sun;
The speech proclaiming the great word in the limitlessness of space is the diamond voice of six syllables;
The mind perfectly staying on the path of space is the great fire of knowledge [and] primordial consciousness;
I bow down to richness till the end of space; grant me clear manifestation of primordial consciousness.

The crown ornament of epistemology are the texts of Dignāga and Dharmakīrti;
The knower of epistemology set up the tradition of explaining them as they are.
This excellent explanation that opens the treasury of epistemology
I offer to the fortunate ones who exert themselves in epistemology.

In this *Elucidation of Meaning of Treasury of Epistemology – the Faultless Commentary on the Intention of Seven Treatises and Sutra* there are two [parts]: establishing the general field of knowledge and ascertaining the essence of valid cognition that perform the act of knowledge. In the first, there are three [subparts]: cognizable object, the mind that performs the act of cognition, the way this mind apprehends the object.

sa bcad

1. *mtshan nyid*

2. *dbye b*a

2.1. gzhan lugs dgag pa

2.2. rang lugs bzhag pa

2.2.1. yul du byes tshul gyi sgo nas yul bzhir dbye ba

2.2.1.1. chos gang yul bzhi 'gyur dpyad pa

2.2.1.2. yul can gang la yul bzhir yod dpyad pa

2.2.1.3. yul bzhi so so'i ngo bo

2.2.1.3.1. snang yul

2.2.1.3.1.1. mtshan nyid

2.2.1.3.1.2. dbye ba

A 2.2.1.3.1.2.1. rtog med shes pa'i snang yul

A 2.2.1.3.1.2.1.1. rnam pa gtad pa'i sgo nas snang yul

A 2.2.1.3.1.2.1.2. rnam pa ma gtad pa'i sgo nas snang yul

A 2.2.1.3.1.2.2. rtog pa'i snang yul

B 2.2.1.3.1.2.1. rang rig mngon sum gyis myang bya

B 2.2.1.3.1.2.2. rtog med log shes la dngos su snang ba'i med pa gsal ba

B 2.2.1.3.1.2.3. rtog pa la dngos su snang ba'i don spyi

2.2.1.3.2. gzung yul

2.2.1.3.2.1. mtshan nyid

2.2.1.3.2.2. dbye ba

2.2.1.3.2.2.1. yul can gyi sgo nas dbye ba

Outline of *Tshad ma rigs pa'i gter gyi don gsal bar byed pa* I

1. Definition

2. Division
  2.1. Refutation of others' systems
  2.2. Presentation of our own system
    2.2.1. Division into four objects from the point of view of the way of making into an object
      2.2.1.1. Analysis of phenomena becoming four objects
      2.2.1.2. Analysis of what are the four objects for a certain subject
      2.2.1.3. The nature of each of the four objects
        2.2.1.3.1. Appearing object
          2.2.1.3.1.1. Definition
          2.2.1.3.1.2. Division
            A 2.2.1.3.1.2.1. Appearing object of nonconceptual cognition
              A 2.2.1.3.1.2.1.1. Appearing object through reference to the aspects
              A 2.2.1.3.1.2.1.2. Appearing object through non-reference to the aspects
            A 2.2.1.3.1.2.2. Appearing object of conceptualization
            B 2.2.1.3.1.2.1. That which is experienced by direct perception as being self-knowledge
            B 2.2.1.3.1.2.2. The nonexistent clearly appearing directly to reverse nonconceptual cognition
            B 2.2.1.3.1.2.3. The object universal directly appearing to conceptualization
        2.2.1.3.2. Apprehended object
          2.2.1.3.2.1. Definition
          2.2.1.3.2.2. Division
            2.2.1.3.2.2.1. Division from the point of view of the subject

2.2.1.3.2.2.1.1. dbang po'i mngon sum gyis gzung yul
2.2.1.3.2.2.1.2. yid kyi mngon sum gyis gzung yul
2.2.1.3.2.2.2. yul gyi sgo nas dbye ba
2.2.1.3.2.2.2.1. gzugs
2.2.1.3.2.2.2.2. sgra
2.2.1.3.2.2.2.3. dri
2.2.1.3.2.2.2.4. ro
2.2.1.3.2.2.2.5. reg bya
2.2.1.3.3. zhen yul
2.2.1.3.3.1. mtshan nyid
2.2.1.3.3.2. dbye ba
2.2.1.3.3.2.1. rtog pa tshad ma'i zhen yul
2.2.1.3.3.2.2. bcad shes kyi zhen yul
2.2.1.3.4. 'jug yul
2.2.1.3.4.1. mtshan nyid
2.2.1.3.4.2. dbye ba
2.2.1.3.4.2.1. mngon sum gyi 'jug yul
2.2.1.3.4.2.1.1. don rig mngon sum gyi 'jug yul
2.2.1.3.4.2.1.2. rang rig mngon sum gyi 'jug yul
2.2.1.3.4.2.1.3. rnal 'byor mngon sum gyi 'jug yul
2.2.1.3.4.2.1.3a. phung po
2.2.1.3.4.2.1.3b. chos nyid
2.2.1.3.4.2.2. rjes dpag gi 'jug yul
2.2.2. ngo bo'i sgo nas bden pa gnyis su dbye ba
2.2.3. 'jug yul gyi sgo nas mngon lkog gnyis su dbye ba
2.2.3.1. mtshan nyid
2.2.3.2. dbye ba
2.2.3.2.1. mngon gyur gyi dbye ba
2.2.3.2.1.1. yul gyi sgo nas dbye ba
2.2.3.2.1.1.1. chos can
2.2.3.2.1.1.1.1. don
2.2.3.2.1.1.1.2. shes pa
2.2.3.2.1.1.2. chos nyid
2.2.3.2.1.2. yul can gyi sgo nas dbye ba
2.2.3.2.1.2.1. rtog med ma 'khrul pa'i sgo nas dbye ba
2.2.3.2.1.2.1.1. don rig mngon sum gyi mngon gyur

2.2.1.3.2.2.1.1. The object apprehended by direct sense perception
2.2.1.3.2.2.1.2. The object apprehended by direct mental perception
2.2.1.3.2.2.2. Division from the point of view of the object
2.2.1.3.2.2.2.1. Physical form
2.2.1.3.2.2.2.2. Sound
2.2.1.3.2.2.2.3. Smell
2.2.1.3.2.2.2.4. Taste
2.2.1.3.2.2.2.5. Touchable
2.2.1.3.3. Conceived object
2.2.1.3.3.1. Definition
2.2.1.3.3.2. Division
2.2.1.3.3.2.1. Conceived object of conceptual valid cognition
2.2.1.3.3.2.2. Conceived object of subsequent cognition
2.2.1.3.4. Object of engagement
2.2.1.3.4.1. Definition
2.2.1.3.4.2. Division
2.2.1.3.4.2.1. The object of engagement of direct perception
2.2.1.3.4.2.1.1. The object of engagement of direct perception as knowledge of an entity
2.2.1.3.4.2.1.2. The object of engagement of direct perception as self-knowledge
2.2.1.3.4.2.1.3. The object of engagement of direct yogic perception
2.2.1.3.4.2.1.3a. Skandhas
2.2.1.3.4.2.1.3b. Phenomenality
2.2.1.3.4.2.2. The object of engagement of inference
2.2.2. Division into two truths from the point of view of the nature
2.2.3. Division into direct and indirect from the point of view of the object of engagement
2.2.3.1. Definition
2.2.3.2. Division
2.2.3.2.1. Division of the direct
2.2.3.2.1.1. Division from the point of view of object
2.2.3.2.1.1.1. The bearer of the quality
2.2.3.2.1.1.1.1. Entity
2.2.3.2.1.1.1.2. Consciousness
2.2.3.2.1.1.2. Phenomenality
2.2.3.2.1.2. Division from the point of view of subject
2.2.3.2.1.2.1. Division from the point of view of non-conceptual non-erroneous cognition
2.2.3.2.1.2.1.1. Direct perception as knowledge of entity

2.2.3.2.1.2.1.2. rang rig mngon sum gyi mngon gyur
2.2.3.2.1.2.1.3. rnal 'byor mngon sum gyi mngon gyur
2.2.3.2.1.2.2. rtog med 'khrul shes kyi sgo nas dbye ba
2.2.3.2.2. lkog gyur gyi dbye ba
2.2.3.2.2.1. yul gyi dbye ba
2.2.3.2.2.1.1. don
2.2.3.2.2.1.2. shes pa
2.2.3.2.2.1.3. chos nyid
2.2.3.2.2.2. yul can gyi dbye ba
2.2.3.2.2.2.1. rjes dpag gi sgo nas dbye ba
2.2.3.2.2.2.1.1. dngos stobs rjes dpag gi lkog gyur
2.2.3.2.2.2.1.2. yid ches rjes dpag gi lkog gyur
2.2.3.2.2.2.1.3. grags pa'i rjes dpag gi lkog gyur
2.2.3.2.2.2.2. tshad min gyi blo'i sgo nas dbye ba
2.2.3.2.2.2.2.1. bcad shes pa'i lkog gyur
2.2.3.2.2.2.2.2. log shes pa'i lkog gyur
2.2.3.2.2.2.2.3. the tshom gyi lkog gyur
2.2.4. 'jug tshul gyi sgo nas rang spyi gnyis su dbye ba
2.2.4.1. mtshan nyid
2.2.4.2. dbye ba
2.2.4.2.1. rang mtshan
2.2.4.2.1.1. don
2.2.4.2.1.1.1. phyi don
2.2.4.2.1.1.2. nang don
2.2.4.2.1.2. shes pa
2.2.4.2.2. spyi mtshan
A 2.2.4.2.2.1. dngos pa la brten pa'i spyi
A 2.2.4.2.2.2. dngos med la brten pa'i spyi
A 2.2.4.2.2.3. gnyis ka la brten pa'i spyi
B 2.2.4.2.2.1. gcig la tha dad du 'byed pa'i spyi
B 2.2.4.2.2.2. tha dad la gcig tu sdud pa'i spyi
B 2.2.4.2.2.3. gcig la gcig tu snang ba'i spyi
B 2.2.4.2.2.4. tha dad la tha dad du snang ba'i spyi
2.2.5. mthar thug gi gzhal bya rang mtshan gcig tu bsdu ba
2.3. rtsod pa spong ba
2.3.1. 'khrul shes yul med la rtsod pa spong ba

2.2.3.2.1.2.1.2. Direct perception as self-knowledge
2.2.3.2.1.2.1.3. Direct yogic perception
2.2.3.2.1.2.2. Division from the point of view of non-conceptual erroneous cognition
2.2.3.2.2. Division of the indirect
2.2.3.2.2.1. Division of the object
2.2.3.2.2.1.1. Entity
2.2.3.2.2.1.2. Consciousness
2.2.3.2.2.1.3. Phenomenality
2.2.3.2.2.2. Division of the subject
2.2.3.2.2.2.1. Division from the point of view of inference
2.2.3.2.2.2.1.1. Indirect of the inference based on the thing
2.2.3.2.2.2.1.2. Indirect of the inference based on trust
2.2.3.2.2.2.1.3. Indirect of the inference based on opinion
2.2.3.2.2.2.2. Division from the point of view of the state of mind that is not valid cognition
2.2.3.2.2.2.2.1. The indirect of subsequent cognition
2.2.3.2.2.2.2.2. The indirect of reverse cognition
2.2.3.2.2.2.2.3. The indirect of doubt
2.2.4. Division into two: particular and universal from the point of view of the way of engagement
2.2.4.1. Definition
2.2.4.2. Division
2.2.4.2.1. Particular
2.2.4.2.1.1. Entity
2.2.4.2.1.1.1. Outer entity
2.2.4.2.1.1.2. Inner entity
2.2.4.2.1.2. Consciousness
2.2.4.2.2. Universal
A 2.2.4.2.2.1. Universality based on thing
A 2.2.4.2.2.2. Universality based on no-thing
A 2.2.4.2.2.3. Universality based on both
B 2.2.4.2.2.1. Universality of the one divided into different ones
B 2.2.4.2.2.2. Universality of different ones reduced to one
B 2.2.4.2.2.3. Universality of the one appearing as one
B 2.2.4.2.2.4. Universality of the different ones appearing as different
2.2.5. Reducing to one – the particular which is the ultimate perceptible
2.3. Rebuttal of objections
2.3.1. Rebuttal of the objection concerning the nonexistence of the object of erroneous cognition

2.3.1.1. gzhal bya gnyis su gsungs ba dang 'gal ba spong ba
2.3.1.2. don spyi dang med pa gsal ba yul du mtshung pa'i rtsod pa spong ba
2.3.1.3. myong ba dang 'gal ba spong ba
2.3.1.4. dgag pa tshad mas mi rtogs par thal ba spong ba
2.3.2. gzung yul rang mtshan la rtsod pa spong ba
2.3.2.1. rtsod pa
2.3.2.2. lan
2.3.2.2.1. grub mtha'i rnam gzhag spyir bstan pa
2.3.2.2.2. gzhan gyis brtags pa dgag pa
2.3.2.2.3. bde bar gshegs pa'i lugs bsgrub pa
2.3.2.2.3.1. dgongs pa ngos gzung ba
2.3.2.2.3.2. de nyid slob dpon gyis ji ltar gtan la phab pa
2.3.2.2.3.2.1. don rig
2.3.2.2.3.2.2. rnam rig

2.3.1.1. Rebuttal of objection concerning the contradiction in claiming two perceptibles

2.3.1.2. Rebuttal of the objection concerning the similarity of objects i.e. the object universal and the nonexistent clearly appearing

2.3.1.3. Rebuttal of the objection concerning contradiction with experience

2.3.1.4. Rebuttal of the entailment that negation is not realized by valid cognition

2.3.2. Rebuttal of the objection concerning the apprehended object as a particular

2.3.2.1. Objection

2.3.2.2. Answer

2.3.2.2.1. The teaching of general presentation of tenets

2.3.2.2.2. Refutation of other [scholars'] analysis

2.3.2.2.3. Proving the Sugata tradition

2.3.2.2.3.1. Identification of the intention

2.3.2.2.3.2. The way it was proven by ācharyas

2.3.2.2.3.2.1. Knowledge of entity

2.3.2.2.3.2.2. Knowledge through the aspect in cognizing consciousness

[yul brtag pa]

<2a/387> shes bya yul|

dang po la gnyis te| mtshan nyid| dbye ba'o||

[1. mtshan nyid]
dang po ni yul gyi mtshan nyid blo'i rig par bya ba| de dang khyab mnyam pa'i shes bya'i mtshan nyid| blo'i yul du byar rung ba| gzhal bya'i mtshan nyid| tshad mas rtogs par bya ba| gzhi grub kyi mtshan nyid| tshad mas dmigs pa| yod nges kyi mtshan nyid| tshad mas bltar rung ba'o||

[2. dbye ba]
gnyis pa la gsum ste|

[2.1] gzhan lugs dgag |
[2.2] rang lugs bzhag |
[2.3] rtsod pa spang ba'o||

[2.1. gzhan lugs dgag pa]
dang po ni bod kha cig snang yul dang| gzung yul don gcig pas <2b/388> don spyi de rtog pa'i gzung yul dang| med pa gsal ba de rtog med log shes kyi gzung yul yin zhes zer ro||
'di dgag pa la rigs pa gnyis las| dang po ni| rtog pa dang rtog med log shes gnyis po chos can| 'khrul shes ma yin par thal| gzung yul can gyi shes pa yin pa'i phyir| gnyis pa ni| don spyi dang med pa gsal ba gnyis po chos can| mthong rung gi yul na gnas pa'i gang zag gzhan gyi shes pas mthong bar thal| rang snang ba'i shes pa las rdzas tha dad pa'i gzung yul yin pa'i phyir|

[Object Analysis]

There are the two in the first [chapter on cognizable object]: [1] definition, [2] division.

[1. Definition]

1. Definition of the object: that which is knowable by mind.[1] Definition of the cognizable having equal scope is that which can be made into an object of mind. Definition of the perceptible is that which is to be realized by valid cognition. Definition of the established basis is that which is observed by valid cognition. Definition of really existent is that which can be seen by valid cognition.[2]

[2. Division]

There are three [subparagraphs] in the second [2]:

[2.1] Refutation of others' systems;

[2.2] Presentation of our own system;

[2.3] Rebuttal of objections.

[2.1. Refutation of others' systems]

Some Tibetans say that since the appearing object and the apprehended object have the same meaning, the universal is the apprehended object of the conceptual [cognition] and the nonexistent clearly [appearing] is the apprehended object of the reverse nonconceptual cognition.[3]

There are two lines of reasoning in the refutation of this [view]. First, the subject matter is both conceptual and nonconceptual reverse cognition; it entails that they are not erroneous cognitions, because they are the cognition having apprehended the object.[4] Secondly, the subject matter is both the universal and the nonexistent clearly [appearing]; it entails that as for the object that can be seen they are seen by cognition of other person nearby, because they are apprehended objects substantially different from the cognition to which they themselves appear.[5]

[2.2. rang lugs bzhag pa]

gnyis pa la lnga ste|

[2.2.1] yul du byas tshul gyi sgo nas yul bzhir dbye ba|
[2.2.2] ngo bo'i sgo nas bden pa gnyis su dbye ba|
[2.2.3] 'jug yul gyi sgo nas mngon lkog gnyis su dbye ba|
[2.2.4] 'jug tshul gyi sgo nas rang spyi gnyis su dbye ba|
[2.2.5] mthar thug gi gzhal bya rang mtshan gcig tu bsdu ba'o||

[2.2.1. yul du byas tshul gyi sgo nas yul bzhir dbye ba]

dang po la gsum ste|

[2.2.1.1] chos gang yul bzhir 'gyur dpyad|
[2.2.1.2] yul can gang la yul bzhir yod dpyad|
[2.2.1.3] yul bzhi so so'i ngo bo'o||

[2.2.1.1. chos gang yul bzhir 'gyur dpyad pa]

dang po ni| chos thams cad yul can gyi blo so so la ltos nas| snang yul| zhen yul| 'jug yul gsum du 'gyur la| gzung yul ni mdo sde pas phyi'i skye mched lnga po kho na la 'jug cing| sems tsam pa'i lugs la gzung yul gyi rnam gzhag med do||

[2.2.1.2 yul can gang la yul bzhir yod dpyad pa]

gnyis pa ni| rtog med ma 'khrul ba'i shes pa thams cad la snang yul yod cing| rtog med 'khrul shes rnams la snang yul med| rtog pa thams cad la snang yul yod do|| gzung yul ni| don rig mngon <3a/389> sum gnyis po kho na la yod cing| zhen yul ni| rtog pa don mthun rnams la yod| 'jug yul ni| tshad ma dang| rjod byed sgra don mthun dang|skyes bu rnams la yod do||

[2.2. Presentation of our own system]
There are five in the second [2.2]:

[2.2.1] Division into four objects from the point of view of the way of making into an object;
[2.2.2] Division into two truths from the point of view of the nature;
[2.2.3] Division into direct and indirect from the point of view of the object of engagement;
[2.2.4] Division into two: particular and universal from the point of view of the way of engagement;
[2.2.5] Reducing to one – the particular which is the ultimate perceptible.

[2.2.1. Division into four objects from the point of view of the way of making into an object]
There are three in the first [2.2.1]:

[2.2.1.1] Analysis of phenomena becoming four objects;
[2.2.1.2] Analysis of what are the four objects for a certain subject;
[2.2.1.3] The nature of each of the four objects.

[2.2.1.1. Analysis of phenomena becoming four objects]
All phenomena being related to individual mind as subject turn out to be an appearing object, a conceived object and an object of engagement. Concerning the apprehended object, Sautrāntika sets up only five external *āyatanas* and in the system of Cittamātra an apprehended object is not maintained.

[2.2.1.2. Analysis of what are the four objects for a certain subject]
All non-erroneous non-conceptual cognitions have an appearing object, whereas erroneous non-conceptual cognitions do not have an appearing object; all conceptualizations have an appearing object.

Concerning the apprehended object, only the two direct perceptions[6] knowing an entity have it.

Concerning the conceived object, conceptualizations that are compatible with an entity thing[7] have it.

Concerning the object of engagement, valid cognition, articulated sound that is compatible with an entity, and sentient beings have it.

[2.2.1.3. yul bzhi so so'i ngo bo]
gsum pa la| snang yul| gzung yul| zhen yul| 'jug yul dang bzhi las|

[2.2.1.3.1. snang yul]
dang po la mtshan nyid dang| dbye ba gnyis|

[2.2.1.3.1.1. mtshan nyid]
dang po ni| des rnam par gtad pa'i sgo nas snang ba'am| rnam med du dngos su snang ba gang rung gyur pa'i yul lo||

[2.2.1.3.1.2. dbye ba]
gnyis pa la| rtog med shes pa'i dang| rtog pa'i snang yul gnyis|

[A]
[A 2.2.1.3.1.2.1. rtog med shes pa'i snang yul]
dang po la rnam pa gtad pa'i sgo nas snang yul du 'gyur ba dang| rnam pa ma gtad pa'i sgo nas snang yul du 'gyur ba gnyis|

[A 2.2.1.3.1.2.1.1. rnam pa gtad pa'i sgo nas snang yul]
dang po ni| don rig mngon sum gyis gzung don lta bu|

[A 2.2.1.3.1.2.1.2. rnam pa ma gtad pa'i sgo nas snang yul]
gnyis pa ni| rang rig mngon sum gyis myang bya lta bu'o||

[A 2.2.1.3.1.2.2. rtog pa'i snang yul]
rtog pa'i snang yul ni don spyi lta bu'o||

[2.2.1.3. The nature of each of the four objects]
There are four in the third [2.2.1.3]:

[2.2.1.3.1] Appearing object;
[2.2.1.3.2] Apprehended object;
[2.2.1.3.3] Conceived object;
[2.2.1.3.4] Object of engagement.

[2.2.1.3.1. Appearing object]
There are two in the first [2.2.1.3.1]: [2.2.1.3.1.1] definition and [2.2.1.3.1.2] division.

[2.2.1.3.1.1. Definition]
It is the following: whatever object that appears by way of bringing out the aspects[8] or that appears directly without aspects.

[2.2.1.3.1.2. Division]
There are two in the second [2.2.1.3.1.2]:

[2.2.1.3.1.2.1] Appearing object of nonconceptual cognition and
[2.2.1.3.1.2.2] [Appearing object] of conceptualization.

[A]
[A 2.2.1.3.1.2.1. Appearing object of nonconceptual cognition]
There are two in the first [A 2.2.1.3.1.2.1]:

[A 2.2.1.3.1.2.1.1] One that is appearing object through reference to the aspects;
[A 2.2.1.3.1.2.1.2] One that is appearing object through non-reference to the aspects.

[A 2.2.1.3.1.2.1.1. Appearing object through reference to the aspects]
The first one is like an entity apprehended by direct perception as being the knowledge of entity [different from it].

[A 2.2.1.3.1.2.1.2. Appearing object through non-reference to the aspects]
Second one is like that which is to be experienced by direct perception as being self-knowledge.

[A 2.2.1.3.1.2.2. Appearing object of conceptualization]
Appearing object of conceptualization is like an object universal.[9]

[B]
yang na yul bzhi'i nang tshan du gyur pa'i snang yul ni yul can gyi shes pa las rdzas gzhan du med cing| rang dus su snang ba la 'jog pa

[B 2.2.1.3.1.2.1] rang rig mngon sum gyis myang bya dang|
[B 2.2.1.3.1.2.2] rtog med log shes la dngos su snang ba'i med pa gsal ba dang|
[B 2.2.1.3.1.2.3] rtog pa la dngos su snang ba'i don spyi gsum po kho na la 'jog cing| bar pa ni shes pa de'i snang yul yin kyang spyir snang yul ma yin zhes pa rigs gter gyi dgongs pa yin nam snyam ste dpyad do||

[2.2.1.3.2. gzung yul]

[2.2.1.3.2.1. mtshan nyid]
gnyis pa la mtshan nyid ni| rang 'dzin mngon sum la rang 'dra'i rnam pa dngos su gtod byed kyi phyi don no||

[2.2.1.3.2.2. dbye ba]
dbye ba|

[2.2.1.3.2.2.1. yul can gyi sgo nas dbye ba]
yul can gyi sgo nas

[2.2.1.3.2.2.1.1] dbang po'i mngon sum gyis gzung yul dang| <3b/390>
[2.2.1.3.2.2.1.2] yid kyi mngon sum gyis gzung yul gnyis|

[2.2.1.3.2.2.2. yul gyi sgo nas dbye ba]
yul gyi sgo nas [2.2.1.3.2.2.2.1] gzugs [2.2.1.3.2.2.2.2] sgra [2.2.1.3.2.2.2.3] dri [2.2.1.3.2.2.2.4] ro [2.2.1.3.2.2.2.5] reg bya lnga'o||

[2.2.1.3.3. zhen yul]
gsum pa la

[2.2.1.3.3.1. mtshan nyid]
mtshan nyid ni| rang 'dzin stangs kyis gtso bor byed pa'i blos zhen nas rig par bya ba|

[B]

Alternatively, among four objects, the appearing object for valid cognition does not exist as a substance that is different from the cognition possessing the object. And when referring to that which appears in its own time, we refer only to three:

> [B 2.2.1.3.1.2.1] that which is experienced by direct perception as being self-knowledge;
> [B 2.2.1.3.1.2.2] the nonexistent clearly appearing directly to reverse [log] nonconceptual cognition;
> [B 2.2.1.3.1.2.3] the object universal directly appearing to conceptualization.

Concerning the second one, even though it is the appearing object of that cognition, generally it is not appearing object, which, I think, is the intention of the *Tshad ma rigs gter*, but it should be [further] analyzed.[10]

[2.2.1.3.2. Apprehended object]

In the second [2.2.1.3.2] there are

[2.2.1.3.2.1. Definition]

Definition: the outer entity directly bringing about the aspect similar to it in the direct perception apprehending it.

[2.2.1.3.2.2. Division]

Division:

[2.2.1.3.2.2.1. Division from the point of view of the subject]

From the point of view of the subject it is [2.2.1.3.2.2.1.1] the object apprehended by direct sense perception and [2.2.1.3.2.2.1.2] the object apprehended by direct mental perception.

[2.2.1.3.2.2.2. Division from the point of view of the object]

From the point of view of the object there are five: physical form [2.2.1.3.2.2.2.1], sound [2.2.1.3.2.2.2.2], smell [2.2.1.3.2.2.2.3], taste [2.2.1.3.2.2.2.4], touchable [2.2.1.3.2.2.2.5].

[2.2.1.3.3. Conceived object]

In the third [2.2.1.3.3] there is

[2.2.1.3.3.1. Definition]

Definition: what is to be known when the conceiving mind makes it important by way of apprehending it.

[2.2.1.3.3.2. dbye ba]
de la dbye na [2.2.1.3.3.2.1] rtog pa tshad ma'i zhen yul dang| [2.2.1.3.3.2.2] bcad shes kyi zhen yul gnyis|

[2.2.1.3.3.2.1. rtog pa tshad ma'i zhen yul]
dang po ni| rjes dpag tshad ma'i 'jug yul rnams so||

[2.2.1.3.3.2.2. bcad shes kyi zhen yul]
gnyis pa ni| tshad ma gnyis kyi 'jug yul de nyid des drangs pa'i bcad shes kyi zhen yul du 'gyur ba lta bu'o||

[2.2.1.3.4. 'jug yul]
bzhi pa la mtshan nyid ni|

[2.2.1.3.4.1. mtshan nyid]
yul can don mthun gyi byed pa 'jug pa'i gzhir gyur pa'i yul gyi gtso bo'o||

[2.2.1.3.4.2. dbye ba]
dbye ba la yul can gyi sgo nas dbye na sngar ltar gsum las dang po tshad ma'i 'jug yul la [2.2.1.3.4.2.1] mngon sum dang| [2.2.1.3.4.2.2] rjes dpag gi 'jug yul gnyis|

[2.2.1.3.4.2.1. mngon sum gyi 'jug yul]
dang po la [2.2.1.3.4.2.1.1] don rig mngon sum gyi 'jug yul ni phyi rol gyi don rang mtshan dang| [2.2.1.3.4.2.1.2] rang rig mngon sum gyi 'jug yul ni shes pa rang mtshan dang| [2.2.1.3.4.2.1.3] rnal 'byor mngon sum gyi 'jug yul ni [2.2.1.3.4.2.1.3a] mdo sde pa ltar na bdag med pas khyad par du byas pa'i phung po rang mtshan dang| [2.2.1.3.4.2.1.3b] rnam rig pa ltar na chos nyid rnams yin na[1]|

[2.2.1.3.4.2.2. rjes dpag gi 'jug yul]
rjes dpag gi 'jug yul ni rtags yang dag gi bsgrub bya rnams la 'jog go|
sgra'i 'jug yul ni ba lang rang mtshan pa de ba lang zhes pa'i sgra don mthun gyi 'jug yul yin pa lta bu'o||

---

[1] In K1, K2 also *na* but should read *no*.

[2.2.1.3.3.2. Division]
Here division is:

[2.2.1.3.3.2.1] Conceived object of conceptual valid cognition;
[2.2.1.3.3.2.2] Conceived object of subsequent cognition.[11]

[2.2.1.3.3.2.1. Conceived object of conceptual valid cognition]
The first are objects of engagement of inferential valid cognition.

[2.2.1.3.3.2.2. Conceived object of subsequent cognition]
The second are like the very objects of engagement of both valid cognitions[12] that become conceived objects of subsequent cognition caused by them.

[2.2.1.3.4. Object of engagement]
In the fourth [2.2.1.3.4] there is

[2.2.1.3.4.1. Definition]
Definition: the main one which is an object that became the basis for engagement making the subject and the entity compatible.

[2.2.1.3.4.2. Division]
Concerning the division, if it is divided from the point of view of the subject, out of three mentioned above, in case of the first one, which is the object of engagement of valid cognition, there are two: [2.2.1.3.4.2.1] the object of engagement of direct perception and [2.2.1.3.4.2.2] the object of engagement of inference.

[2.2.1.3.4.2.1. The object of engagement of direct perception]
In the case of the former one [2.2.1.3.4.2.1.1] the object of engagement of direct perception as knowledge of an entity is the outer entity as the particular; and [2.2.1.3.4.2.1.2] the object of engagement of direct perception as self-knowledge is cognition as the particular; and [2.2.1.3.4.2.1.3] the object of engagement of direct yogic perception according to Sautrāntika is [2.2.1.3.4.2.1.3a] the particular which is skandhas specified by selflessness[13] and according to aspectarians is [2.2.1.3.4.2.1.3b] phenomenalities.[14]

[2.2.1.3.4.2.2. The object of engagement of inference]
The object of engagement of inference is referred to as that which is to be proven through authentic reason.

The object of engagement of the sound is like the ox being the particular that is the object of engagement of compatibility between the sound "ox" and the entity.

[2.2.2. ngo bo'i sgo nas bden pa gnyis su dbye ba]

gnyis pa'i ngo bo'i sgo nas bden pa gnyis la| bye brag tu[2] smra bas bcom pa'am blos gzhig pa na der 'dzin gyi blo mi 'jug pa de kun rdzob bden pa'i mtshan nyid de| dper na bcom pa na de 'dzin gyi blo mi 'jug pa bum pa lta bu <4a/391> dang| blos rdul rdzas brgyad so so phye pa na der 'dzin gyi blo mi 'jug pa 'jig rten grags pa'i chu lta bu'o||

bcom pa'am blos gzhig pa na der 'dzin gyi blo 'jug pa de don dam bden pa'i mtshan nyid de| dper na gzugs kyi skye mched lta bu'o zhes 'dod de| mdzod las|

> gang la bcom dang blo yis gzhan||
> bsal na de blo mi 'jug pa||
> bum chu bzhin du kun rdzob tu||
> yod de don dam yod gzhan no||* zhes gsungs pa'i phyir ro||

mdo sde pas| don dam par don byed nus pa dang mi nus pa'i chos gnyis de gnyis kyi mtshan nyid du 'dod de| don dam don byed nus pa gang|** |zhes sogs gsungs pa'i phyir|

sems tsam pas| gang la dngos su dmigs nas kun nas nyon mongs pa rgyas su rung ba de kun rdzob bden pa'i mtshan nyid dang| gang la dngos su dmigs nas rnam byang rgyas pas khyab pa de don dam bden pa'i mtshan nyid du bzhed de| kun btus las|

> gang la dmigs nas kun nas nyon mongs 'phel bar[3] 'gyur ba'i dmigs pa ni kun rdzob tu yod pa'o|| gang la dmigs nas rnam par byung ba 'phel bar 'gyur ba'i dmigs pa ni don dam du yod pa'o|| zhes gsungs pa'i phyir|

dbu ma pas| mthong ba yang dag pa'i 'dzin stangs kyis gzung bya de don dam bden pa'i mtshan nyid de| dper na 'phags rgyud kyi mnyam gzhag gi 'dzin stangs kyis gzung bya lta bu'o|| mthong ba brdzun pa'i 'dzin stangs kyis gzung bya de kun rdzob bden pa'i mtshan nyid de| dper na so skye'i blo'i <4b/392> dngos yul lta bu zhes bzhed de| 'jug pa las|

---

* A 6.5.

** PV III 3a: arthakriyāsamarthaṃ yat.

[2] K1: *tu* omitted.

[3] K1: par

[2.2.2. Division into two truths from the point of view of the nature]
In the case of the two truths from the point of view of the nature, according to Vaibhāṣika, when something is destroyed or inquired into by the mind, then that nonengagement of the mind apprehending it is the definition of the truth of complete projection. For example, it is like the vase that the mind apprehending it is not engaged into when it is destroyed, and it is like the water known to the world the mind apprehending it is not engaged into when it is analyzed by the mind in terms of particular eight atomic substances.[15]

When something is destroyed or inquired into by the mind, that engagement of the mind apprehending it is the definition of absolute truth. For example, it is like the āyatana of form as it is accepted, for it is said in *Abhidharmakośa*:

> If something is destroyed or excluded intellectually
> Mind does not engage into it.
> It exists as complete projection as vase or water.
> The absolute exists the other way.[16]

Sautrāntika holds that the definitions of the two are two phenomena: the one that is effective on the absolute [level] and the one that is not,[17] since it is said that "the absolute is whatever is effective,"[18] etc.

Cittamātra maintains that the definition of the truth of complete projection is whatever thoroughly increases afflictions while being really perceived, and the definition of absolute truth is whatever necessarily increases complete purity while being really perceived.[19] Since in *Abhidharmasamuccaya* it is said:

> The perceived [object] that thoroughly expands afflictions while being perceived, exists as complete projection. The perceived [object] that expands complete purity while being perceived, exists as absolute.[20]

Madhyamaka mantains that the definition of absolute truth is that which is apprehended by the apprehension seeing really. For example, it is like that which is apprehended by the apprehension of the ārya's mind-stream in equipoise. The definition of the truth of complete projection is that which is apprehended by the apprehension seeing falsely.[21] For example the real object of the mind of the ordinary being.[22] As it is said in *Madhyamakāvatāra*:

dngos kun yang dag brdzun par mthong ba yis||
dngos rnyed bgo bo gnyis ni 'dzin par 'gyur||
yang dag mthong yul gang de de nyid de||
mthong ba rdzun pa'ang kun rdzob bden par gsungs||* zhes gsungs pas so||

[2.2.3. 'jug yul gyi sgo nas mngon lkog gnyis su dbye ba]
gsum pa 'jug yul gyi sgo nas mngon lkog gnyis la [2.2.3.1] mtshan nyid dang| [2.2.3.2] dbye ba gnyis|

[2.2.3.1. mtshan nyid]
dang po mtshan nyid la don spyi la ma ltos par rtogs par bya ba dang| don spyi'i sgo nas rtogs par bya ba'o||

[2.2.3.2. dbye ba]
gnyis pa dbye ba la| [2.2.3.2.1] mngon gyur gyi dbye ba dang| [2.2.3.2.2] lkog gyur gyi dbye ba gnyis|

[2.2.3.2.1. mngon gyur gyi dbye ba]
dang po la [2.2.3.2.1.1] yul gyi sgo nas dbye ba dang| [2.2.3.2.1.2] yul can gyi sgo nas dbye ba gnyis las|

[2.2.3.2.1.1. yul gyi sgo nas dbye ba]
dang po la [2.2.3.2.1.1.1] chos can dang| [2.2.3.2.1.1.2] chos nyid gnyis|

[2.2.3.2.1.1.1. chos can]
dang po la [2.2.3.2.1.1.1.1] don dang [2.2.3.2.1.1.1.2] shes pa gnyis so||

[2.2.3.2.1.2. yul can gyi sgo nas dbye ba]
yul can gyi sgo nas dbye ba la| [2.2.3.2.1.2.1] rtog med ma 'khrul pa'i sgo nas dang| [2.2.3.2.1.2.2] rtog med 'khrul shes kyi sgo nas dbye ba gnyis las|

---

* M6.23.

Since all things are seen really and falsely,
There is the apprehension of two natures: real and false.
Any object seen really is suchness;
And what is seen falsely is complete projection, as [Buddha] said.[23]

[2.2.3. Division into direct and indirect from the point of view of the object of engagement]

Concerning the two: the direct and indirect from the point of view of the object of engagement there is:

[2.2.3.1] Definition and
[2.2.3.2] Division.

[2.2.3.1. Definition]

The definition is what is to be realized without referring to the object universal and what is to be realized through the object universal.

[2.2.3.2. Division]

The division is into:

[2.2.3.2.1] Division of the direct;
[2.2.3.2.2] Division of the indirect.[24]

[2.2.3.2.1. Division of the direct]

Here are the two:

[2.2.3.2.1.1] Division from the point of view of object;
[2.2.3.2.1.2] Division from the point of view of subject.

[2.2.3.2.1.1. Division from the point of view of object]

Here are the two:

[2.2.3.2.1.1.1] The bearer of quality [*chos can*]
[2.2.3.2.1.1.2] Phenomenality.

[2.2.3.2.1.1.1. The bearer of quality]

Here there are [2.2.3.2.1.1.1.1] the [outer] entity and [2.2.3.2.1.1.1.2] consciousness.

[2.2.3.2.1.2. Division from the point of view of subject]

Division from the point of view of subject is twofold:

[2.2.3.2.1.2.1] Division from the point of view of non-conceptual non-erroneous [cognition];
[2.2.3.2.1.2.2] Division from the point of view of non-conceptual erroneous cognition.

[2.2.3.2.1.2.1. rtog med ma 'khrul pa'i sgo nas dbye ba]
dang po la [2.2.3.2.1.2.1.1] don rig mngon sum| [2.2.3.2.1.2.1.2] rang rig mngon sum| [2.2.3.2.1.2.1.3] rnal 'byor mngon sum la mngon gyur dang gsum las|

[2.2.3.2.1.2.1.1. don rig mngon sum gyi mngon gyur]
dang po ni| gzugs sogs don lnga'o||

[2.2.3.2.1.2.1.2. rang rig mngon sum gyi mngon gyur]
gnyis pa ni shes pa thams cad do||

[2.2.3.2.1.2.1.3. rnal 'byor mngon sum gyi mngon gyur]
gsum pa ni chos nyid lta bu'o||

[2.2.3.2.1.2.2. rtog med 'khrul shes kyi sgo nas dbye ba]
gnyis pa ni| zla gnyis de zla ba gnyis snang gi dbang shes la mngon gyur yin pa lta bu'o||

[2.2.3.2.2. lkog gyur gyi dbye ba]
gnyis pa lkog gyur gyi dbye ba la [2.2.3.2.2.1] yul dang [2.2.3.2.2.2] yul can gyi dbye ba gnyis las|

[2.2.3.2.2.1. yul gyi dbye ba]
dang po la sngar ltar gsum las|

[2.2.3.2.2.1.1] dang po ni bum pa de bum 'dzin rtog pa la lkog gyur yin pa dang|

[2.2.3.2.2.1.2] shes pa ni rang rgyud kyi shes pa de gzhan sems shes pa'i mngon shes med pa'i gang zag la lkog gyur <5a/393> yin pa dang|

[2.2.3.2.2.1.3] chos nyid so skye la lkog gyur yin pa lta bu'o||

[2.2.3.2.1.2.1. Division from the point of view of non-conceptual non--erroneous cognition]

Here are three direct ones in:

[2.2.3.2.1.2.1.1] direct perception as knowledge of entity;
[2.2.3.2.1.2.1.2] direct perception as self-knowledge;
[2.2.3.2.1.2.1.3] direct yogic perception.

[2.2.3.2.1.2.1.1. Direct perception as knowledge of entity]

the first one is five entities such as form etc.;

[2.2.3.2.1.2.1.2. Direct perception as self-knowledge]

the second one is all cognitions;

[2.2.3.2.1.2.1.3. Direct yogic perception]

the third one is phenomenality.

[2.2.3.2.1.2.2.] Division from the point of view of non-conceptual erroneous cognition]

They are like two moons being the direct for the sense consciousness of the appearing of two moons.[25]

[2.2.3.2.2. Division of the indirect]

Division of the indirect is done into

[2.2.3.2.2.1] Division of the object and
[2.2.3.2.2.2] Division of the subject.

[2.2.3.2.2.1. Division of the object]

Here are the three above mentioned like that:

[2.2.3.2.2.1.1] The first one is the vase that is the indirect for the conceptualization apprehending the vase.

[2.2.3.2.2.1.2] Concerning consciousness, it is the consciousness of one's own mindstream that is the indirect for the person who does not have direct cognition of other mind's consciousness.

[2.2.3.2.2.1.3] Phenomenality is the indirect for ordinary beings.

[2.2.3.2.2.2. yul can gyi dbye ba]
yul can gyi sgo nas dbye ba la| [2.2.3.2.2.2.1] rjes dpag gi sgo nas dbye ba dang| [2.2.3.2.2.2.2.] tshad min gyi blo'i sgo nas dbye ba gnyis las|

[2.2.3.2.2.2.1. rjes dpag gi sgo nas dbye ba]
dang po la [2.2.3.2.2.2.1.1] dngos stobs rjes dpag [2.2.3.2.2.2.1.2] yid ches rjes dpags [2.2.3.2.2.2.1.3] grags pa'i rjes dpags la lkog gyur gsum ni gtan tshigs gsum po de'i bsgrub bya lta bu'o||

[2.2.3.2.2.2.2. tshad min gyi blo'i sgo nas dbye ba]
gnyis pa la [2.2.3.2.2.2.2.1] bcad shes| [2.2.3.2.2.2.2.2] log shes| [2.2.3.2.2.2.2.3] the tshom la lkog gyur dang gsum las|

[2.2.3.2.2.2.2.1. bcad shes pa'i lkog gyur]
dang po ni| sngon po de sngo 'dzin dbang mngon gyis drangs pa'i nges shes la lkog gyur yin pa lta bu'o||

[2.2.3.2.2.2.2.2. log shes pa'i lkog gyur]
gnyis pa ni sgra rtag pa de sgra rtag 'dzin rtog pa la lkog gyur yin pa lta bu'o||

[2.2.3.2.2.2.2.3. the tshom gyi lkog gyur]
gsum pa ni sgra rtag mi rtag gang rung de de ltar the tshom za ba po'i the tshom mngon gyur pa la de yin pa lta bu'o||

des na rtog med ltog shes la mngon gyur yin na mngon gyur yin pas ma khyab cing| rtog pa log shes la lkog gyur yin na lkog gyur yin pas ma khyab ste| rtog med log shes kyi snang yul yin na yod pas ma khyab pa'i phyir dang| rtog pa log shes kyi zhen yul yin na yod pas ma khyab pa'i phyir| the tshom la lkog gyur yin pa la ni don la gnas pa'i phyogs rnams lkog gyur yin la| cig shog ni lkog gyur ma yin no||

[2.2.3.2.2.2 Division of the subject.]
Division from the point of view of the subject is done into

[2.2.3.2.2.2.1] Division from the point of view of inference;
[2.2.3.2.2.2.2] Division from the point of view of the state of mind that is not valid cognition.[26]

[2.2.3.2.2.2.1. Division from the point of view of inference]
There are three indirects for [2.2.3.2.2.2.1.1] the inference based on the thing, [2.2.3.2.2.2.1.2] inference based on trust, and [2.2.3.2.2.2.1.3] inference based on opinion – they are what is proven in these three argumentations.

[2.2.3.2.2.2.2. Division from the point of view of the state of mind that is not valid cognition]
There are three indirects as

[2.2.3.2.2.2.2.1] [Object of] subsequent cognition;[27]
[2.2.3.2.2.2.2.2] [Object of] reverse cognition;[28]
[2.2.3.2.2.2.2.3] [Object of] doubt.[29]

[2.2.3.2.2.2.2.1. Object of subsequent cognition]
Like the blue [colour], which is the indirect of the reliable cognition caused by direct sense perception apprehending [it] earlier.

[2.2.3.2.2.2.2.2. Object of reverse cognition]
Like the permanent sound, which is the indirect for the conceptualization apprehending permanent sound.

[2.2.3.2.2.2.2.3. Object of doubt]
Like a direct doubt of somebody doubting whether sound is permanent or impermanent.

Therefore if there is something that is the direct for reverse non-conceptual cognition, it would not necessarily be the direct; and if there is something that is the indirect in case of reverse conceptual cognition, it would not necessarily be the indirect. This is because if there is something that is an appearing object of the reverse nonconceptual cognition, it is not necessarily an existent, and because if there is something that is a conceived object of reverse conceptual cognition, it is not necessarily an existent. In the case of that which is the indirect of the doubt, some parts of the entity are indirect and the others are not indirect.

[2.2.4. 'jug tshul gyi sgo nas rang spyi gnyis su dbye ba]
bzhi pa 'jug tshul gyi sgo nas rang spyi gnyis la| [2.2.4.1] mtshan nyid dang| [2.2.4.2] dbye ba gnyis las|

[2.2.4.1. mtshan nyid]
dang po ni rim bzhin| yul dus rang bzhin ma 'dres par gnas pa'i dngos po dang| yul dus rang bzhin thun mong bar snang ba'i sgro btags <5b/394> so|| yang na thun mong ma yin par gnas pa'i dngos po dang| thun mong bar snang ba'i sgro btags te| rnam nges las|

> de ni thun mong ma yin par gnas pa'i dngos po'i rang bzhin te| rang gi mtshan nyid do||*

ces gsungs pa'i dngos shugs gnyis las shes so||

[2.2.4.2. dbye ba]
gnyis pa|

[2.2.4.2.1. rang mtshan]
rang mtshan la dbye na| [2.2.4.2.1.1] don dang [2.2.4.2.1.2] shes pa rang mtshan gnyis|

[2.2.4.2.1.1. don]
dang po la [2.2.4.2.1.1.1] phyi don bem po dang| [2.2.4.2.1.1.2] nang don bem po gnyis|

[2.2.4.2.1.1.1. phyi don]
dang po la| gzugs sogs phyi'i skye mched lnga|

[2.2.4.2.1.1.2. nang don]
gnyis pa la mig sogs nang gi skye mched lnga'o||

---

* PVin 1.153.1.

[2.2.4. Division into two: particular and universal from the point of view of the way of engagement]

In the case of particular and universal from the point of view of the way of engagement there is

[2.2.4.1] Definition and
[2.2.4.2] Division.

[2.2.4.1. Definition]

Respectively, [the first one is] the thing that stays autonomous in terms of object, time, essence[30] and [the second is] imputation appearing as common in terms of object, time, essence. Or else, the thing staying as uncommon and imputation appearing as common, since in *Pramāṇaviniścaya* it is said:

> They are the essence of the thing staying as uncommon;
> And the particular itself.[31]

So [the topic] is known in both ways: directly [from Dharmakīrti][32] and indirectly [from Go rams pa].[33]

[2.2.4.2. Division]

[2.2.4.2.1. Particular]

If the particular is divided, there are

[2.2.4.2.1.1] the particular which is an entity and
[2.2.4.2.1.2] the particular which is consciousness.

[2.2.4.2.1.1. Entity]

Here there is

[2.2.4.2.1.1.1] The matter which is an outer entity and
[2.2.4.2.1.1.2] The matter which is an inner entity.

[2.2.4.2.1.1.1. Outer entity]

Here there are five outer āyatanas like the form etc.

[2.2.4.2.1.1.2. Inner entity]

Here there are five inner āyatanas like the eye etc.

[2.2.4.2.1.2. shes pa]

shes pa rang mtshan la dbye na| rnam par shes pa tshogs drug 'khor dang bcas pa yod do||

[2.2.4.2.2. spyi mtshan]

spyi mtshan la dbye ba| bod snga rabs pa rnams| ldog pa med dgag gi spyi dang| blo'i gzhan sel ba'i spyi gnyis gsungs kyang| gzhung las bshad pa ni|

> [A 2.2.4.2.2.1] dngos po dang| [A 2.2.4.2.2.2] dngos med dang|
> [A 2.2.4.2.2.3] gnyis ka la brten pa'i spyi gsum ste|
> dngos dang dngos med gnyis ka la||
> brten phyir spyi de'ang rnam pa gsum||[*] zhes gsungs pa'i phyir|

yang [B 2.2.4.2.2.1] gcig la tha dad du 'byed pa'i spyi| [B 2.2.4.2.2.2] tha dad la gcig tu sdud pa'i spyi| [B 2.2.4.2.2.3] gcig la gcig tu snang ba'i spyi| [B 2.2.4.2.2.4] tha dad la tha dad du snang ba'i spyi dang bzhir dbyer rung ste| gzhan sel la de ltar phye ba gang zhig spyi dang spyi mtshan gzhan sel gsum gnad gcig pa'i phyir ro||

[2.2.5. mthar thug gi gzhal bya rang mtshan gcig tu bsdu ba]

lnga pa mthar thug gi gzhal bya rang mtshan gcig tu bsdu ba ni| 'o na| rang gi mtshan nyid gcig gzhal bya||[**] zhes sogs gzhal bya rang mtshan gcig tu gsungs pa'i don ji ltar snyam <6a/395> na| spyir rtog ge'i gshung lugs las| dang po grub mtha' la zhugs ma zhugs thams cad la grags pa'i tshad ma ngos bzungs nas| de dang 'dra ba'i ston pa tshad ma'i skyes bur bsgrub pa skabs kyi don yin te| mi bslu ma shes don gsal ngos bzung nas| de'i 'og tu| de ldan bcom ldan tshad ma nyid||[***] ces gsungs pa'i phyir| grub mtha' la zhugs ma zhugs thams cad la grags pa tshad ma'i don ni| rnam nges las| phan pa dang mi phan pa thob pa dang spong ba ni nges par yang dag pa'i shes pa sngon du 'gro ba can yin pas[****] zhes pa'i skabs nas bstan pa ltar phan gnod nus pa'i yul la blang dor byed pa'i rgyur gyur pa'i shes pa yin la| de lta bu'i tshad mas blang bya'i phan pa nus pa'i yul dang| dor bya'i gnod par nus pa'i yul ni rang mtshan kho na yin te| rang mtshan kho nas phan gnod nus kyi spyi mtshan gyis de mi nus pa'i phyir te|

---

[*] PV III 51: yathoktaviparītaṃ yat tat svalakṣanam iṣyate | sāmānyaṃ trividhaṃ tac ca bhāvābhāvaubhayāśrayāt ||

[**] PV III 53d: meyaṃ tv ekaṃ svalakṣaṇam ||

[***] PV II 7a: tadvat pramāṇaṃ bhagavān

[****] PVin 1.152.3.

[2.2.4.2.1.2. Consciousness]

If the particular which is consciousness is divided, there are six groups of conditioned consciousness and the related ones.[34]

[2.2.4.2.2. Universal]

If the universal is divided, previous Tibetan thinkers said that there are two: the universality of the exclusion[35] which is non-implicative negation[36] and the universality of intellectual *apoha*.[37] However the explanation in the texts says that:

> there are three universalities based on [A 2.2.4.2.2.1] thing, [A 2.2.4.2.2.2] non--thing and [A 2.2.4.2.2.3] both; the universalities and also the three aspects are there because they are based on thing, non-thing and both.[38]

Or else there can be division into four:
[B 2.2.4.2.2.1] Universality of the one divided into different ones;
[B 2.2.4.2.2.2] Universality of different ones reduced to one;
[B 2.2.4.2.2.3] Universality of the one appearing as one;
[B 2.2.4.2.2.4] Universality of the different ones appearing as different.
This is because similar divisions are made in case of *apoha*, since universality, universal and apoha have the same meaning.[39]

[2.2.5. Reducing to one – the particular that is the ultimate perceptible]

Concerning reducing to one – the particular which is the ultimate perceptible – if you think what it means to say that the perceptible is particular only as in [quotation] "Particular only [is] the perceptible,"[40] then generally according to the tradition of texts on reasoning it means that first after identifying what is known as valid cognition for the ones that have philosophical system and the ones who do not have, there comes the moment for proving that the teacher similar to that is the embodiment of valid cognition; because after identifying that [valid cognition is] non-deceptive clarifying of the entity not known before, later it is said that "Bhagavan that has it is valid cognition itself."[41] Concerning the meaning of what is known as valid cognition for everyone who is engaged in a philosophical system and who is not, *Pramāṇaviniścaya* says: "Concerning achieving what is beneficial and abandoning what is not beneficial, one starts with reliable and true cognition."[42] And it is shown that it is cognition that becomes the cause for adopting and rejecting the objects that can bring benefit and harm. In this way the object that can bring benefit and is to be adopted by valid cognition and the object that can bring harm and is to be abandoned are exclusively the particular since what is exclusively particular can bring benefit and harm while the universal can not do this. As it is said:

> de ni blang dor 'bras can pas||
> skyes bu thams cad 'jug pa yin||[4]

zhes dang|

> don byed nus pa ma yin la||
> don gnyer brtags pas ci zhig bya||[*] zhes gsungs pa'i phyir dang|

rang mtshan gcig nyid la don rig mngon sum 'jal byed du 'jug pa'i tshe gzung yul dang| rjes dpags 'jal byed du 'jug pa'i tshe zhen yul yin la| tshad ma de gnyis la brten nas skyes bu 'jug pa'i tshe mi bslu bas na 'jug yul yin te| 'di la dgongs nas| rigs gter rang 'gral las|

> rang mtshan de nyid dngos su 'jal na gzung yul yin la|| lkog gyur du <6b/396> 'jal na zhen yul la yin cing| gnyis ka yang skyes bu 'jug na mi bzlu bas 'jug yul yin no|| zhes gsungs so||

dngos su 'jal na zhes pa'i don yang mngon gyur du 'jal na zhes pa'i don yin pa tshig grogs kyi stobs kyis shes so||
mdor na rang mtshan gcig nyid la tshad ma mngon rjes gnyis 'jal byed du 'jug pa'i tshe 'jug tshul gyi gzhal bya la rang spyi gnyis su yod kyang 'jug yul gyi[5] gzhal bya rang mtshan kho na yin pa ni| rang gi mtshan nyid gcig gzhal bya|| zhes sogs kyi dgongs pa 'khrul pa med pa ste| lha'i 'grel par|

> de ltar na rang gi mtshan nyid kho na rang gi ngo bo dang| gzhan gyi ngo bo'i sgo nas rtogs pa'i phyir| de dag gi mtshan nyid ci 'dra pa[6] dang| gzhal bya gnyis nyid du rnam par gzhag nas zhes gsungs so||

---

[*] PV I 211 ab: arthakriyāsamarthasya vicāraiḥ kiṃ tadarthinām |
[4] PVin 1.173.4.
[5] K1: *'jug yul gyi* omitted.
[6] K1, K2: ba

> Since what is to be accepted and abandoned have consequences, all beings engage into them,[43]

and

> Why to pursue and investigate the object that is not effective?[44]

It is only the particular which, when comprehended by direct perception that is the knowledge of the entity, is the apprehended object. When it is comprehended by direct inference, it is the conceived object. Based on these two valid cognitions at the time when the being engages into it, there is object of engagement because of nondeceptiveness. Concerning the intention here auto-commentary to the *Tshad ma rigs gter* says:

> If one thoroughly perceives this very particular, it is the apprehended object. If one perceives the indirect, it is the conceived object. And if somebody is engaged in both as well, then since they they are objects of engagement because of non-deceptivness.[45]

The meaning of the phrasing "thoroughly perceives" and also what is the meaning of phrasing "evidently perceives" is known through the modifier.[46]

In short, when valid cognition engages only in comprehending the particular by way of direct perception and inference, then even though the perceptible is twofold from the point of view of the way of engaging, namely, particular and universal, only the particular as an object of engagement is the perceptible. This is non-erroneous intention of the phrase "particular only [is] the perceptible."[47] As it is said in the commentary of Devendrabuddhi:

> Since it is only the particulars which can be comprehended from the point of view of their own nature and of the other, how can they be defined? [They are presented] by way of two perceptibles.[48]

[2.3. rtsod pa spong ba]

gsum pa rtsod pa spong ba la gnyis te| [2.3.1] 'khrul shes yul med la rtsod pa spong ba dang| [2.3.2] gzung yul rang mtshan la rtsod pa spong ba'o||

[2.3.1. 'khrul shes yul med la rtsod pa spong ba]

dang po la bzhi ste| [2.3.1.1] gzhal bya gnyis su gsungs pa dang 'gal ba spong ba| [2.3.1.2] don spyi dang med pa gsal ba yul du mtshungs pa'i rtsod pa spong ba| [2.3.1.3] myong ba dang 'gal ba spong ba| [2.3.1.4] dgag pa tshad mas mi rtogs par thal ba spong ba'o||

[2.3.1.1. gzhal bya gnyis su gsungs pa dang 'gal ba spong ba]

dang po ni| rang mtshan gcig nyid la mngon rjes gnyis 'jal byed du 'jug pa'i tshe 'jug yul rang mtshan kho na yin na| slob dpon phyogs glang gis gzhal bya gnyis su gsungs pa dang 'gal lo zhe na| skyon med de| rang mtshan gcig nyid rang gi ngo bo'i sgo nas rtogs pa dang| gzhan don spyi'i sgo nas rtogs pa'i rtogs tshul <7a/397> gnyis yod pas rang spyi gnyis su bzhag pa yin pa'i phyir|

[2.3.1.2. don spyi dang med pa gsal ba yul du mtshungs pa'i rtsod pa spong ba]

gnyis pa ni| don spyi don la med kyang gzhal bya yin na| med pa gsal ba yang de dang mtshungs so zhe na| skyon med de| snga ma ni rang mtshan ma yin yang de la brten nas 'jug yul rang mtshan thob pa yod cing| phyi ma ni rang gi ngo bo rang mtshan ma yin cing| de la brten nas 'jug yul rang mtshan thob pa yang med pa'i phyir|

[2.3. Rebuttal of objections]

There are two [paragraphs] in the rebuttal of objections:

[2.3.1] Rebuttal of the objection concerning the nonexistence of the object of erroneous cognition,

[2.3.2] Rebuttal of the objection concerning the apprehended object as a particular.

[2.3.1. Rebuttal of the objection concerning the nonexistence of the object of erroneous cognition]

Here are four:

[2.3.1.1] Rebuttal of objection concerning the contradiction in claiming two perceptibles,

[2.3.1.2] Rebuttal of the objection concerning the similarity of objects i.e. the object universal and the nonexistent clearly [appearing],

[2.3.1.3] Rebuttal of the objection concerning contradiction with experience,

[2.3.1.4] Rebuttal of the entailment that negation is not realized by valid cognition.

[2.3.1.1. Rebuttal of objection concerning the contradiction in claiming two perceptibles]

If someone says: "If at the time of engaging by way of comprehending exclusively the particular by the two: direct perception and inference, the apprehended object is only a particular, then there is contradiction, with acarya Dignāga claiming that there are two perceptibles," there is no fault [in our system]. This is because there are the two posited – particular and universal, since there are two ways of comprehending: from the point of view of own nature only a particular is comprehended and the other is comprehended from the point of view of the object universal.[49]

[2.3.1.2. Rebuttal of the objection concerning the similarity of objects i.e. the object universal and the nonexistent clearly appearing]

If someone says: "If object universal – despite its nonexistence in reality – is a perceptible, then also nonexistent clearly [appearing] is similar to it," there is no fault [in our system]. This is because concerning the first one [object universal], even though it is not a particular, on the basis of it the object of engagement, which is the particular, is obtained,[50] and concerning the second one [nonexistent clearly appearing] its own nature is not the particular and [therefore] on the basis of it object of engagement, which is the particular, is not obtained at all.[51]

[2.3.1.3. myong ba dang 'gal ba spong ba]
gsum pa ni| snang yul rang mtshan ma yin na| shes pa la gsal bar snang ba dang 'gal lo zhe na| skyon med de| rtog pa la gsal bar snang ba'i rnam pa'i cha dang| de la phyi rol du sgra btags pa'i cha gnyis las| dang po ni| shes pa dang| phyi ma ni| spyi mtshan yin pa'i phyir ro||

[2.3.1.4. dgag pa tshad mas mi rtogs par thal ba spong ba]
bzhi pa ni| dngos med 'jal byed kyi tshad ma med par thal| blang dor byed pa'i rgyur gyur pa'i tshad ma'i 'jug yul yin na| rang mtshan yin dgos pa'i phyir zhe na| skyon med de| dngos med 'jal byed kyi tshad ma yod med dpyod par byed pa'i phyir| de dag gi don rigs gter las| yul gnyis bzhed pas gnod ce na|| zhes pa nas bsgrub pa'i phyir na 'gal ba med|| ces pa'i bar gyi tshigs bcad phyed dang lnga'i don ma 'khrul bar bshad zin to||

[2.3.2. gzung yul rang mtshan la rtsod pa spong ba]
gnyis pa la| [2.3.2.1] rtsod pa dang| [2.3.2.2] lan gnyis las|

[2.3.2.1 rtsod pa]
dang po ni| gzung yul gyi gzhal bya rang mtshan gcig tu 'dod pa mi 'thad de| phyi rol don du gyur ba'i gzung yul mkhas pas bkag |shes par gyur pa'i gzung yul 'dir mi srid pa'i phyir ro zhes pa'o||

[2.3.2.2. lan]
gnyis <7b/398> pa la| [2.3.2.2.1] grub mtha'i rnam gzhag spyir bstan pa dang| [2.3.2.2.2] gzhan gyis brtags pa dgag pa| [2.3.2.2.3] bde bar gshegs pa'i lugs bsgrub pa dang gsum las|

[2.3.2.2.1. grub mtha'i rnam gzhag spyir bstan pa]
dang po ni| mu stegs ngo bo nyid rgyur smra ba rnams kyis ngo no nyid rgyur 'dod pa dang| dbang phyug pa rnams kyis dbang phyug rgyur 'dod pa dang| grags

[2.3.1.3. Rebuttal of the objection concerning contradiction with experience]
If someone says: "If the appearing object is not the particular, it contradicts the fact that it appears clearly to the cognition," there is no fault [in our system]. This is because there are two parts: the part of the aspect appearing clearly to conceptualization and the part of projection referring to it as external. Out of these two the first one is cognition and the second is the universal.

[2.3.1.4. Rebuttal of the entailment that negation is not realized by valid cognition]
If someone says: "It entails nonexistence of valid cognition comprehending a non-thing, since the object of engagement of the valid cognition is the object that becomes the cause for performing accepting and rejecting, so it must be a particular," there is no fault [in our system]. This is because of the [aforementioned] analysis whether there is or is not valid cognition comprehending non--thing. The meaning of that it is explained non-erroneously by the four and a half stanzas of the *Tshad ma rigs gter* from "If to say that, since [Dignāga] accepts two objects, it invalidates [Sa skya Paṇḍita's position]" to "since you prove [...], there is no contradiction."[52]

[2.3.2. Rebuttal of the objection concerning the apprehended object as a particular]
Here are the two:

[2.3.2.1] Objection;
[2.3.2.2] Answer.

[2.3.2.1. Objection]
It is said: "It is not admissible to accept that the perceptible which is apprehended object is the particular only. This is because the wise one negated the apprehended object being an outer entity [and] here [in the *Tshad ma rigs gter*] it is not possible for the apprehended object to be the one that is cognized."

[2.3.2.2. Answer]
There are three:

[2.3.2.2.1] The teaching of general presentation of tenets;
[2.3.2.2.2] Refutation of other [scholars'] analysis;
[2.3.2.2.3] Proving the Sugata tradition.

[2.3.2.2.1. The teaching of general presentation of tenets]
Non-Buddhists [*Tīrthikas*] who say that the nature is the cause claim the nature as a cause.[53] Followers of Īśvara claim Īśvara as a cause. Sāṃkhya claims *prakṛti* as

can pa rnams kyis gsto bo rgyur 'dod pa dang| gzegs zan dang| nyan thos sde gnyis kyis rdul kyis rdul phran der 'dod pa dang| sems tsam pas snang ba thams cad sems su 'dod pa dang| ngo bo nyid med par smra bas chos thams cad don dam spros pa dang bral ba dang| kun rdzob tu dngos smra ba de dag dang mtshungs kyang rung 'dzin rten gyu grags pa dang mtshungs kyang rung bar bzhed do||

[2.3.2.2.2. gzhan gyis brtags pa dgag pa]

gnyis pa ni| ngo bo nyid rgyur 'dod pa ni mi 'thad de| rgyu med las skye ba 'gog pa'i rigs pas gnod pa'i phyir| dbang phyug dang gtso bo rgyur 'dod pa yang mi 'thad de| rtag pa las skye ba 'gog pa'i rigs pas gnod pa'i phyir|

[2.3.2.2.3. bde bar gshegs pa'i lugs bsgrub pa]

gsum pa la| [2.3.2.2.3.1] dgongs pa ngos gzung ba dang| [2.3.2.2.3.2] de nyid slob dpon gyis ji ltar gtan la phab pa dang gnyis las|

[2.3.2.2.3.1. dgongs pa ngos gzung ba]

dang po ni| bde bar gshegs pas tha snyad la 'jug pa'i tshe rdul phran zhal gyis bzhes la| 'di la bye brag smra ba dang| mdo sde pa'i grub mtha' gnyis yod do| tha snyad kyi de kho na nyid la 'jug pa'i tshe sems tsam zhal gyis bzhes la| 'di la rnam bden brdzun gnyis yod do|| don dam pa'i de kho na nyid la 'jug pa'i tshe chos thams cad spros pa dang bral ba la 'jug par mdzad do||

[2.3.2.2.3.2. de nyid slob dpon gyis ji ltar gtan la phab pa]

gnyis pa ni| de ltar sangs <8a/399> rgyas pa'i grub mtha' bzhi las| slob dpon gyis gang gtan la dbab pa yin zhe na| 'di la [2.3.2.2.3.2.1] don rig dang| [2.3.2.2.3.2.2] rnam rigs gnyis las|

[2.3.2.2.3.2.1. don rig]

dang po khas len pa'i tshe| bye brag tu smra bas dbang shes kyis rang dang dus mnyam pa'i phyi don rnam med rjen char du 'dzin par 'dod pa de bkag nas skad cig snga mar rkyen gsum tshogs pa las skad cig gnyis par dbang shes yul gyi rnam ldan du skyes pa tsam la phyi don rtogs par 'dod pa mdo sde pa'i grub mtha' zhal gyis bzhes te| slob dpon nyid kyi zhal nas| gal te phyi rol dpyod la 'jug pa na|| kho bos mdo sde'i skabs la rnam par brten|| zhes gsungs par grags so||

cause.[54] Leftovers eaters[55] and two Śrāvaka schools[57] claim atoms as it [a cause]. Cittamātrins claim that all appearances are mind. Niḥsvabhāvavādins[57] admit that all dharmas are on the absolute [level] free from projections and that on the relative [level] they are acceptable as being similar either to Vastusatpadārthavādins [Śrāvaka] or to worldly opinions.[58]

[2.3.2.2.2. Refutation of other scholars' analysis]

Claiming that nature is the cause is not admissible since it is undermined by the argumentation refuting creation without the cause. Claiming Īśvara and *prakṛti* as cause is also not admissible since it is undermined by the argument refuting creation from the permanent.[59]

[2.3.2.2.3. Proving the Sugata tradition]

Here are the two:

[2.3.2.2.3.1] Identification of the intention and
[2.3.2.2.3.2] The way it was proven by ācharyas.

[2.3.2.2.3.1. Identification of the intention]

When addressing conventions sugata proclaimed atoms; and there are two systems – that of Vaibhāṣika and that of Sautrāntika. When addressing thatness of the conventional, he proclaimed Cittamātra. Concerning that there are two [systems], that of true and false aspects. When addressing thatness of the absolute, he referred to all dharmas as free from projections.

[2.3.2.2.3.2. The way it was proven by ācharyas]

Thus out of these four Buddhist systems, which one was settled by ācharyas? Concerning this question there are two

[2.3.2.2.3.2.1] Knowledge of entity;[60]
[2.3.2.2.3.2.2] Knowledge through an aspect [in cognizing consciousness].[61]

[2.3.2.2.3.2.1. Knowledge of entity]

When accepting [the system of knowledge of the outer entity] he rejected the claim of Vaibhāṣika, that the sense consciousness apprehends directly without aspects the outer entity simultaneous with it. Then he proclaimed the system of Sautrāntika, which claims the cognition of the outer entity in the way that after three conditions[62] coming together in the first moment in the second moment there is only sense consciousness born having an aspect. As it is known from the words of ācarya himself: "If engaging in analysis of the outer [object], I fully rely on the level of Sautrāntika."[63]

[2.3.2.2.3.2.2. rnam rigs]

gnyis pa| rnam rig zhal gyis bzhes pa'i tshe rnam bden pas dbang shes la rags par snang ba bden grub tu 'dod pa de bkag nas rnam med zhal gyis bzhes te|

> de phyir don dang shes pa la|
> rags snang yod min* zhes sogs gsungs pa'i phyir|

des na skabs 'dir mdo sems gyis las| gong du smras pa'i rtsod pa de mdo sde pa'i dbang du byes pa yin na| gtan tshigs dang po ma grub ste| de'i lugs la rnam pa gtod byed kyi phyi don nyid gzung yul du 'jog pa'i phyir ro||
sems tsam pa'i dbang du byas na 'dod pa yin te| de'i lugs la gzung yul gyi dbang du byas pa'i yul dang yul can grub pa med pa'i phyir| don 'di la dgongs nas| rigs gter du|

> ji srid phyi rol khas len pa|| de srid rgyu la gzung yul zer|| shes bya nang gir zhugs pa na|| yul <8/b400> dang yul can grub pa med|| ces gsungs so||

yul brtag pa'i rab tu byed pa ste dang po bzhad zin to|| ||

* PV III 211ab: tasmān na artheṣu na jñāne sthūlabhāsas tadātmanaḥ |

[2.3.2.2.3.2.2. Knowledge through the aspect in cognizing consciousness]

At the time of proclaiming of knowledge through the aspect, he rejected the claim of true aspectarians that gross appearances are truly established within sense consciousness and proclaimed lack of aspects, since it is said:

> Thus entity and consciousness do not exist as gross appearances.[64]

So then there are two [traditions] here: Sautrāntika and Cittamātra. If the above formulated objection is treated by way of Sautrāntika, the first argumentation[65] does not hold because in this tradition the outer entity referred to through the aspect is referred to as an apprehended object.

If it is treated by way of Cittamātra, [the same] is claimed, since in this tradition the subject and object got on the basis of apprehended object is not established. That is why in the *Tshad ma rigs gter* it is said:

> As long as the outer is accepted, for that long the cause is said to be an apprehended object. If what is to be cognized is posited as inside one, object and subject are not established.[66]

The explanation of the first chapter being the "Object Analysis" is completed.

Notes

[1] Remark on the rewording of the definition of cognizable object from the *Tshad ma rigs gter* cf. footnote 14 in Introduction.

[2] As Dreyfus comments: "in this view, the perception of an object does not materially constitute that object. Rather, it is only the necessary and sufficient condition for our being able to determine that the object exists. When we say ajar is in the room, we are implying that this is so because we correctly perceive such a jar, regardless of whether our perception has created the object or not. Thus, the definition of *existence* in terms of being an object of valid cognition is not an idealist statement about how the world is constituted. Rather, it reflects an analysis of our ordinary usage of words such as 'is' and 'exists.' Such a definition is accepted by Buddhist epistemologists as a way to relate ontological and epistemological inquiries, regardless of whether they are idealists." Dreyfus (1997: 76).

[3] Discussion on reverse cognition cf. Introduction.

[4] Go rams pa, following Sa skya Paṇḍita, points out the paradoxical, and thus unwanted consequence of the assumption that erroneous cognition really apprehends an object. Cf. discussion in the Introduction.

[5] The discussion of this argument cf. Stoltz (2006).

[6] Two out of four direct perceptions are meant here, namely direct sense perception [*dbang po mngon sum*] and direct mental perception [*yid mngon sum*].

[7] What is meant here is the inferential cognition that refers correctly to the object that really exists when the representation in the mind is accurate.

[8] In original *rnam pa* which is the translation of Sanskrit *ākāra.* Concerning the meaning of the term in Indian and particularly in Buddhist philosophy cf. Kellner (2014). Cf. also McClintock (2014) and Moriyama (2014).

[9] Discussion on the term *don spyi* cf. Introduction.

[10] Cf. discussion in the introduction.

[11] Subsequent cognition [*bcad shes*] is briefly characterized by Sa skya Paṇḍita as follows: "Subsequent cognition is recollection of what is past [*bcad shes 'das pa dran pa yin*]." T1 78. Go rams pa gives the following definition: "Definition of subsequent cognition: "knowledge engaging in the object that has been realized before and is kept intact [in memory] which is knowledge contradicting projections that are opposite to it [object] [*bcad shes kyi mtshan nyid/ sngar rtogs zin gyi byed pa ma nyams pa'i don la/ log phyogs kyi sgro 'dogs dang 'gal bar 'jug pa'i rig pa*]." G 51. Dreyfus summarizes Sa-paṇ's critique of this concept introduced by Phya pa chos kyi seng ge: "Sa-paṇ grants that subsequent cognition exists, but does not accept it as a division of nonvalid cognition. For Sa-paṇ, subsequent cognitions are nonrealizing cognitions. He rejects the idea that subsequent cognitions have any cognitive role. They merely repeat a previous cognition without contributing to the identification of an object. Hence, it is not even a realization of a previously realized object, as Ge-luk thinkers would have it. Sa-paṇ compares the identification of an already cognized object to cutting a tree already cut." Just as something that is already established and not forgotten does not need to be reestablished, something previously understood cannot be understood unless one forgets it in the meanwhile.

Sa-paṇ is particularly critical of the idea of the second moment of a perception as a subsequent cognition. Since perception merely holds its object and since this object is in constant transformation, the subsequent moments of perception are as valid as the first moment. Therefore, no perception can ever be a subsequent cognition. Only the conceptions that are recollections (*dran shes*) of something previously realized can be subsequent cognitions." Dreyfus (1997: 391).

[12] Direct perception and inference.

[13] More on this topic cf. John D. Dunne saying: "In practice, the Buddhist adept is meant to realize all four aspects of that truth, and one such aspect is impermanence, especially as applied to the psychophysical aggregates (*skandha*). Certainly, on Dharmakīrti's system the constituents that make up the aggregates can be considered causally efficient, ultimately real particulars. Nevertheless, the impermanence of those particulars is not ultimately real. Instead, as with any quality applied to that which possesses it, impermanence is formed through a process of abstraction and exclusion. That is, a quality such as impermanence is conceptually abstracted from the particulars it qualifies, but in ontological terms, that quality is reducible to the particulars themselves." Dunne (2006: 509).

[14] The conception of three natures [*mtshan nyid gsum*] is meant here. Among these three natures there are two that are considered as phenomenality or absolute truth, namely *yongs su grub pa* and one type of *gzhan gyi dbang*, which is pure [*dag pa'i gzhnan dbang*]. The other two: *ma dag pa'i gzhan dbang* and *kun brtags* are considered to be the truth of complete projection [*kun rdzob*].

I decided to translate *chos nyid* as "phenomenality" to preserve in English the affinity from Sanskrit and Tibetan between *dharma* [*chos*] as phenomenon and *dharmatā* [*chos nyid*] in the sense of absolute truth [*don dam bden pa*].

[15] The eight atomic substances [*rdul rdzas brgyad*] according to abhidharmic philosophy are divided into two groups. The first group encompasses the earth atom [*sa rdul*], water atom [*chu rdul*], fire atom [*me rdul*] and the wind atom [*rlung rdul*]. The second one encompasses the ones based on the previous four: the form atom [*gzugs rdul*], smell atom [*dri rdul*], taste atom [*ro rdrul*] and the atom of the touchable [*reg bya'i rdul*].

[16] A18 [6.5]. Concerning the relation of Vasubandhu and Buddhist epistemology after Dignāga, Arnold says that the latter "retains the basic intuition underlying Vasubandhu's approach: the idea that there are two fundamentally different kinds of things (the reducible and the ontologically basic) and that the "two truths" (or, emphasizing *sat* rather than *satya,* two kinds of existents) should be understood as consisting of two sets of enumerable entities. Now, however, it is not *dharmas* that are said to constitute the set of "ultimately existent" (*paramārthasat*) phenomena, but *svalakṣaṇas*. And where Vasubandhu had (in keeping with the conventional sense of the Sanskrit word) understood *svalakṣaṇas* as definitions individuating *dharmas* as *categories*, *svalakṣaṇas* are now viewed as the unique, discrete phenomena that are the direct objects of perceptual cognition – such that *svalakṣaṇas* here would correspond to what had been, for Vasubandhu, the potentially innumerable tokens of the type *dharma*. These ontological primitives are, moreover, here defined particularly by their being causally efficacious – which means (in terms of the epistemological concerns of this program) by their capacity in particular to cause perceptual cognitions." Arnold (2005: 28).

[17] Cf. summary of Sautrāntika theory: "Given the theory of causality, the idea of spatiotemporal restriction then serves to positively establish the entire Sautrāntika system:

1) Whatever exists, occupying space and time, is produced (*kṛtaka*) or conditioned (*saṃskṛta*) by a cause, because spatiotemporal restriction is impossible without a cause.
2) A conditioned, individual and impermanent thing is able to produce an effect through restricting the effect to a particular place and time (*deśakālaniyama*) in accordance with its own spatiotemporal location. [=x', y' and z']
3) A pervasive and permanent thing, if it existed, could not produce an effect because it would be unable to restrict the effect to a particular place and time; this is because it would have no spatiotemporal location of its own.

From this theory of causality, one can derive the ontological distinction between the individual and the universal, and thus the theory of momentariness, in the following way:

1) Only the individual (*svalakṣaṇa*) is causally efficacious (*arthakriyāsamartha*) and therefore ultimately real (*paramārthasat*). A pervasive and permanent thing such as the universal (*sāmānya*) is causally inefficacious and therefore not existent in reality (*asat*).
2) Because a pervasive and permanent or non-momentary thing does not exist in reality due to its lack of causal efficacy, all existents are exclusively impermanent (*anitya*) or momentary (*kṣaṇika*)." Yoshimizu (2007: 1073–1074).

[18] PV III 3a.

[19] In *Yogācārabhūmi* [T31: 1610.793c25–794a2.] the two truths in the context of three natures in yogācāra are described as follows: "We can say neither that the two truths exist, nor that they do not exist, because they are neither existent nor nonexistent. As for the fact that we cannot say that the ultimate truth exists or does not exist: 1) we cannot say that [the ultimate truth] exists, because there are no persons or dharmas; [but] 2) we cannot say that [the ultimate truth] does not exist, because of the demonstration of the emptiness of the two [i.e., persons and dharmas]. The same is true of the conventional truth. Because of its imagined nature, we cannot say that [the conventional truth] exists. Because of its dependent nature, we cannot say that it does not exist. Moreover, the ultimate truth is not definitely existent or nonexistent. Persons and dharmas do not exist, and yet they are not nonexistents. The emptiness of the two [i.e., persons and dharmas] exists, and yet it is not existent. The same is true of the conventional truth. It is not definitely nonexistent because of its imagined nature. Nor is it definitely existent because of its dependent nature." [tr. Zhihua Yao cf. Yao (2014: 324)]

[20] AS p. 56 [I].

[21] In *Madhyamakāvatāra* also the following explanation is given: "Ignorance obscures the essence, hence complete projection. Whatever it brings about seems to be true. *Muni* calls it truth of complete projection. The things brought about [this way] are complete projection [*gti mug rang bzhin sgrib phyir kun rdzob ste| |des gang bcos ma bden par snang de ni| |kun rdzob bden zhes thub pa des gsungs te| |bcos mar gyur pa'i dngos ni kun rdzob tu'o||*]." MA 6.28.

[22] The real object meant here is of course the object that is held as real by deluded perception. Within deluded perception one can distinguish proper apprehension and erroneous apprehension. As it is explained in *Madhyamakāvatāra*: "It is maintained that that false seeing has two aspects: the one with clear faculties and the one with defective faculties. Cognition comming from defective is considered false in relation to cognition coming from proper faculties. What is held by six faculties that are free from flaws, is what is realized by worldly beings. For worldly beings they are true. The rest, according to worldly beings, is mistaken, they claim [*mthong ba brdzun pa'ang rnam pa gnyis 'dod de| |dbang po gsam dang dbang po skyon ldan no| |skyon ldan dbang can rnams kyi shes pa ni| |dbang po legs gyur shes ltos log par 'dod| |gnod pa med pa'i dbang po drug rnams kyis| |gsung ba gang zhig 'jig rten gyis rtogs te| |'jig rten nyid las bden yin lhag ma ni| |'jig rten nyid las log par rnam par bzhag|*]." Cf. MA 6.24–25.

[23] MA 6.23.

[24] Cf. note 27 to translation of *Tshad ma rigs gter*.

[25] Cf. discussion of this example in the introduction.

[26] The definition given by Go rams pa is the following: "Concerning the first one, it is cognition that is not non deceptive [*mi bslu ba ma yin pa'i shes pa*]." Przybyslawski (2016: 402).

[27] Cf. note 10 above.

[28] The definition given by Go rams pa is the following: "The cognition that is apprehending completely it's object based either on seeing its own object clearly or through contrary premise [*'gal rtags*] but is invalidating taking its own object as something it is not." Przybyslawski (2016: 404). Cf. discussion of this definition in the notes 31 and 32 there.

[29] The definition given by Go rams pa is the following: "it is the conceptualization that apprehends it but while uninterruptedly performing apprehension of that it is possible that it will apprehend that it is not [like] that." Przybyslawski (2016: 406). Cf. Dreyfus (1997: 389–391).

[30] Yoshimizu discusses this definition as follows: "Go ram pa's definition of rang mtshan (Skt. svalakṣaṇa) also seems to have been accepted by earlier Tibetans. In fact, the expression *yul dus rang bzhin ma 'dres pa* is so well established among Tibetan scholars that one can hardly find a different formulation in their definitions of rang mtshan, despite the fact that there is no equivalent among Indian authors for the words *ma 'dres pa*, which mean "do not share" or "do not mix up." Tracing the original source of this new formulation is a difficult task. PV III 2 aside, Dharmakīrti himself, it is true, often uses the expression "not mixed up" (*miś* or *saṃ-sṛj* for "mixed up") to describe the essential uniqueness of the individual, but never in the sense of sharing or not sharing place and time. Sa skya Paṇḍita Kun dga' rgyal mtshan (1182–1251), in his auto-commentary to the *Rigs gter*, also speaks of the nature of individuals as being substances that do not mutually mix (*rdzas phan tshun ma 'dres pa*), but he does not also mention spatiotemporal location." Yoshimizu (2007: 1068). More on that topic cf. Yoshimizu (2007: 1067–1069).

[31] PVin 1.153.1.

[32] According to Sa skya Paṇḍita, claiming to follow Dharmakīrti of course, these crucial notions are understood as follows: "Apprehending of a particular is nonconceptual. Apprehending of the universal is conceptual. Here particular is the thing and universal is that which does not exist as object established. The so called particular itself, individuals, thing, substance, the isolated, the absolute, etc. are established as the ones that are effective, substance, as unmixed with other, as cause and result. They are what is to be accepted and what is to be abandoned into which normal beings engage or withdraw from. So since they are the object of engagement, they have the same meaning as the thing. [...]

The universal, apoha, the reverse, devoid of aspects, non-autonomous, related – the so called relative etc. – do not stay within absolute. They are not established as any object. Not being the object of sense, they are projections of the mind. [*rang mtshan 'dzin pa rtog med de/ spyi 'dzin pa ni rtog pa yin/ de la rang mtshan dngos po ste/ spyi ni dngos por grub pa med/ rang gi mtshan nyid gsal ba dngos po rdzas log pa don dam pa zhes bya ba la sogs pa ni don byed nus pa rdzas phan tshun rna 'dres pa rgyu dang 'bras bur grub pa skye bu thams cad kyi blang dor bya ba'i 'jug yul yin pas dngos po don du don gcig pa yin te/* [...] *spyi dang/ gzhan sel dang/ ldog pa dang/ rnam gcos dang/ 'drel pa dang/ 'brel pa dang/ kun rdzob ces bya ba la sogs pa ni/ don la mi gnas pa/ dngos por ma gdub pa/ dbang po'i yul ma yin pa blos sgro brtags pa/*]." T1 85n.

[33] Cf. discussion of Go rams pa's understanding of *rang mtshan* in: Yoshimizu (2007: 1067–1069). Also cf. Yoshimizu (2004: 117–133); Dreyfus (1997: 67–82, 90–94, 111–118).

[34] In other words, the division is made into the so called main mind [*gtso sems*], including all the above mentioned six consciousnesses [*mig gi rnam par shes pa, rna ba'i rnam par shes pa, sna'i rnam par shes pa, lce'i rnam par shes pa, lus kyi rnam par shes pa, yid kyi rnam par shes pa*] and mental acts [*sems byung*] which are called '*khor* – the ones related [to the main mind].

[35] Go rams pa refers here to the *dge lugs* system in which *ldog pa*, as Tillemans explains, functions it the context of realism: "although objects of thought, such as universal, *sādhya* etc., are themselves no more than mind-created appearances/representations (*snang ba* = *pratibhāsa*) or exclusions (*ldog pa* = *vyāvṛtti*), it does not follow that if *x* is such an object of thought, *x* is mind-created – real particulars can be said to be the ascertained objects (*nges yul*), or equally, to use the words of dGe 'dun grub pa and lCang skya rol pa'i rdo rje, they are the explicit objects (*dngos yul*) of thought; elsewhere in Tsong kha pa and virtually all other dGe lugs pa writers on the matter, it is routinely mentioned that they actually appear (*snang ba*) to thought." Tillemans (1999: 216). Compare also Tillemans (1999: 222–224).

The term *ldog pa* in Sa skya tradition is understood in the following way (note that Dreyfus translates *ldog pa* as distinguisher): "Only individuals (*gsal ba, vyakti*) are real. Thus universals, being universally characterized phenomena and not specific individuals, can be only unreal. They are conceptual characteristics (known as *distinguishers, ldog pa, vyāvṛtti*) through which we categorize things. The reason universally characterized phenomena are unreal is they do not meet the three sets of identity conditions delineated by Dharmakīrti. Śākya Chok-den, for example, defines a universal as 'that unique distinguisher which is the mere preclusion of [things of] discordant kinds.' A universal is a distinguisher; that is, it is not a real property but a negatively constructed one. For example, the universal cowness is not some essential property that all cows would share but merely the exclusion of all cows from a class (non-cow) to which they do not belong." Dreyfus (1997: 154).

[36] Concerning non-implicative negation [*prasajyapratiṣedha, med dgag*] Avalokitavrata says: "This [*prasajyapratiṣedha*] has the following characteristics: (1) it does not show the sign of *arthāpatti*; (2) is devoted to negation, aims only at negation, i.e. simply negates what is asserted by the other party; (3) does not affirm the existence of an entity or non-entity; (4) having [the characteristic of] negation and without having [those of] implication and the affirmation of an entity, expresses [the object of negation] by its own word, as when one, meaning 'not a Brahman' says 'not a Brahman' by which he simply makes negation." Quotation translated in: Kajiyama (1973: 170).

[37] According to Go rams pa one of the possible divisions of *apoha* is into *apoha* referring to existence [*yod pa gzhan sel*] and *apoha* referring to non-existence [*med pa gzhan sel*]. The first one is further divided into sound *apoha* [*sgra'i gzhan sel*] and intellectual *apoha* [*blo'i gzhan sel*]; Cf. his *sde bdun mdo dang bcas pa'i dgongs pa phin ci ma log par 'grel ba tshad ma rigs pa'i gter gyi don gsal bar byed pa* in: *dpal sa skya pa'i tshad ma rig pa'i gzhung gces bsdus*, G 71. More on Sa skya Paṇḍita's typology of *apoha* cf. also Hugon (2008: 223–238). Tillemans' remark quoted in note 10.

[38] PV III 51. As Dreyfus says, "Sa-gya thinkers seem to be on stronger grounds when they argue that realism is unsound as an interpretation of Dharmakīrti's ideas. Go-ram-ba denounces one of the main Ge-luk interpretive moves: that which differentiates universal (*spyi, sāmānya*) and universally characterized phenomena (*spyi mtshan, sāmānyalakṣana*). No such distinction is ever made by Dharmakīrti, argues Go-ram-ba. On the contrary, Dharmakīrti repeatedly identifies these two. For example, Dharmakīrti specifies three types of universally characterized phenomena: 'Since they rely on either thing, nonthing, [or] both, these universals are also threefold.' This division serves as a typology of both universals and universally characterized phenomena. It suggests no difference between the two. Therefore, their separation is without solid basis in Dharmakīrti's system. Universals can be no more real than universally characterized phenomena." Dreyfus (1997: 157).

[39] As Dreyfus says, "Sa-paṇ provides a parallel list for the conceptual domain of universally characterized phenomena: universal (*spyi, sāmānya*), elimination of others (*gzhan sel, anyāpoha*), distinguisher (*ldog pa, vyāvṛtti*), preclusion (*rnam gcod, vyavaccheda*), indeterminate (literally 'mixed,' *'dres pa*), relation (*'brel ba, sambandha*), relative (*kun rdzob, saṃvṛti*). These phenomena do not exist in reality (*don la mi gnas pa*) for they are superimposed (*sgro btags pa*) by thought." Dreyfus (1997: 77).

[40] PV III 53d.

[41] PV II 7a. Concerning interpretation of this verse and Buddha as embodiment of valid cognition in Dharmakīrti, cf. van Bijlert (1989: 115–120, 158–168). Also cf. Ruegg (1994); Silk (2002); Steinkellner (1983).

[42] PVin 1.152.3.

[43] PVin 1.173.4.

[44] PV I 211ab.

[45] T1 53 (autocommentary to 11c).

[46] *tshig grogs* – literally "accompanying word," technical term of Tibetan grammar referring to words modifying or enriching the meaning of the words they accompany. Adjectives, adverbs etc. are included into this category. Here the terms "thoroughly" and "evidently" are meant.

[47] PV III 53d.

[48] D 144.

[49] Cf. discussion in the introduction and also Dreyfus (1997: 78).

[50] Sa skya Pandita and Go rams pa in this case follow Dharmakīrti. Cf. Dreyfus (1997: 74).

[51] In other words nonexistent clearly appearing is not effective, it does not perform any function.

[52] The fragment mentioned is as follows: "They say, if [Dignāga] accepts two objects, it invalidates [Sa skya Paṇḍita's position that there is only one]. From the point of view of the way of engagement there are two: particular and universal. If they say that even nonexistent is similar to the perceptible, then concerning this, there can't be any purpose for that object. Appearance such as a strand of hair etc. is mind itself. Appearance as a strand of hair is not established as an object. So if to analyze whether it exists as an object or does not exist, it is universal. If they say: both nonexistent things object universal and nonexistent clearly appearing are established together with self-knowing and that is why they are clear, then both mistaken cognitions have no object but because they are experienced by self-knowing, they are cognitions themselves. Moreover because of apprehending non-being, they are mistaken cognitions. If they say, if there is no object that is a particular, the nonexistence of the object contradicts the perceptible, then since you prove whether what is to be rejected is the existing or nonexisting object, there is no contradiction [*yul gnyis bzhed pas gnod ce na/ /'jug tshul sgo nas rang spyi gnyis/ /med pa'ang gzhal byar mtshungs she na/ /de la yul gyi dgos nus med/ /skra soTa snang ba blo nyid yin/ /skrar snang don la grub pa med/ /de ni dngos por yod med ces/ /rtog pas dpyod na spyi mtshan yin/ /dngos med gnyis po rang rig gi/ /shugs la grub pas gsal zhe na/ /'khrul shes gnyis la yul med cing/ /rang rig gis ni myong ba'i phyir/ /shes pa nyid yin de yang ni/ /med pa 'dzin phyir 'khrul shes yin/ /rang mtshan min pa'i yul med na/ /dngos med gzhal byar 'gal zhe na/ /dgag bya dngos por yod med ces/ /bsgrub pa'i phyir na 'gal ba med/*]." T1 11d–15.

[53] Cf. note 69 in the translation of *Tshad ma rigs gter.*

[54] The view of Sāṃkhya is summarized by Shaw as follows: "The Sāṃkhya philosophers claim that the effect in its subtle form is present in the cause or the set of causal conditions. In other words, the effect in its essence is not different (*abheda*) from its cause or causal conditions. In the Sāṃkhya philosophy, the word 'production' does not mean 'creation of a totally new object.' Similarly, 'destruction' does not mean 'total cessation of an object.' Everything is a manifestation of Nature called '*prakṛti*.' Instead of the word 'production' or 'creation' the Sāṃkhya philosophers use the expression 'manifestation' or 'appearance.' Similarly, instead of 'destruction' or 'cessation' they prefer the word 'disappearance.' No one denies that causality involves change, but the Sāṃkhya philosophers interpret change as a state from unmanifest to manifest or from manifest to unmanifest. Īśvarakṛṣṇa in his *Sāṃkhyakārikā* has put forward five arguments in favour of the view that the effect is real or exists (*sat*) in some form even before its production. Hence the word 'appearance' is more appropriate than 'creation.'" Shaw (2002: 215).

[55] Cf. note 57 in the translation of *Tshad ma rigs gter.*

[56] Vaibhāṣika and Sautrāntika are meant here.

[57] The term refers to both Madhyamaka schools, namely, Svātantrika and Prāsaṅgika.

[58] Cf. note 59 in the translation of *Tshad ma rigs gter.*

[59] *Locus classicus* for these critiques are of course first chapter of *Mūlamadhyamakakārikā*, sixth chapter of *Madhyamakāvatāra* [*dbu ma la 'jug pa*], cf. also *Śūnyatāsaptati* 1–6. Cf. note 61 to the translation of *Tshad ma rigs gter.*

[60] Cf. note 55 in the translation of *Tshad ma rigs gter*.

[61] The conditions meant here are: objective condition [*mig rkyen*] being the thing perceived, subjective condition [*bdag rkyen*] being the sense organ, and immediate condition [*de ma thag rkyen*] being the mind.

[62] Cf. note 85 in the translation of *Tshad ma rigs gter.*

The question of Sautrāntika view in Dharmakīrti's philosophy was quite extensively discussed in Western literature. Cf. Arnold (2008); Dreyfus (1997: 85–87, 99–105, 380–385); Dunne (2004: 58–95, 70–74); Kellner (2011).

[63] PV III 211ab.

[64] The argumentation presented in 2.3.2.

[65] T1 68.

GLOSSARY

TIBETAN	ENGLISH
kun rdzob	– complete projection
rkyen	– condition
lkog gyur	– indirect
skad cig ma	– momentary
khyab pa	– pervasion
‘khrul ba	– erroneous
grangs can pa	– Sāṃkhya
grub mtha’	– tenet
dgag pa	– refutation
‘gal ba	– contradiction
rgyu	– cause
rgyu mtshan	– reason
sgra	– sound
sgra spyi	– sound universal
sgrub pa	– establish
sgro btags	– imputation
bsgrub bya	– what is to be proven
nges	– ascertain
ngo bo	– nature
dngos po	– thing
dngos med	– non-thing
mngon gyur	– direct
mngon sum	– direct perception
bcad shes	– subsequent cognition

chos – phenomenon
chos can – subject
chos nyid – phenomenality

'jug yul – object of engagement
rjes dpag – inference

gtan tshig – argumentation
rtags – reason
rtog pa – conceptual
rtog med – non-conceptual

tha snyad – convention

don – entity
don dam – absolute
don spyi – object universal
don byed nus pa – effective
don rig – knowledge of entity
bdag – self
bdag nyid – nature
bdag med – selflessness
rdul phran – atom

rnam pa – aspect
rnam rig – knowledge through the aspect
rnam shes – conditioned consciousness
snang ba – appearance
snang yul – appearing object

dpe – example
spang pa – rebuttal
spyi – universality
spyi mtshan – universal

bye brag pa – Vaiśeṣika
blo – mind
dbang po – sense faculty
'bras bu – effect
'brel ba – relation

ma 'khrul ba – non-erroneous

tshad ma – valid cognition
mtshan nyid – definition

rdzas – substance

zhen yul – conceived object
gzhal bya – perceptible

gzung yul – apprehended object

yul – object
ye shes – primordial consciousness

rang mtshan – particular
rang bzhin – essence
rang rig – self-knowledge

shes pa – consciousness, cognition
shes bya – cognizable
sems – mind
sems tsam – Cittamātra

ENGLISH TIBETAN

absolute – don dam
appearance – snang ba
appearing object – snang yul
apprehended object – gzung yul
argumentation – gtan tshig
ascertain – nges
aspect – rnam pa
atom – rdul phran

cause – rgyu
Cittamātra – sems tsam
cognizable – shes bya
complete projection – kun rdzob

conceived object – zhen yul
conceptual – rtog pa
condition – rkyen
conditioned consciousness – rnam shes
consciousness, cognition – shes pa
contradiction – 'gal ba
convention – tha snyad

definition – mtshan nyid
direct – mngon gyur
direct perception – mngon sum

effect – 'bras bu
effective – don byed nus pa
entity – don
erroneous –'khrul ba
essence – rang bzhin
establish – sgrub pa
example – dpe

imputation – sgro btags
indirect – lkog gyur
inference – rjes dpag

knowledge of entity – don rig
knowledge through the aspect – rnam rig

mind – blo, sems
momentary – skad cig ma

nature – bdag nyid, ngo bo
non-conceptual – rtog med
non-erroneous – ma 'khrul ba
non-thing – dngos med

object – yul
object of engagement – 'jug yul
object universal – don spyi

particular – rang mtshan
perceptible – gzhal bya

pervasion – khyab pa
phenomenon – chos
phenomenality – chos nyid
primordial consciousness – ye shes

reason – rgyu mtshan, rtags
rebuttal – spang pa
refutation – dgag pa
relation –'brel ba

Sāṃkhya – grangs can pa
sense faculty – dbang po
self – bdag
self-knowledge – rang rig
selflessness – bdag med
sound – sgra
sound universal – sgra spyi
subject – chos can
subsequent cognition – bcad shes
substance – rdzas

tenet – grub mtha'
thing – dngos po

universal – spyi mtshan
universality – spyi

Vaiśeṣika – bye brag pa
valid cognition – tshad ma

what is to be proven – bsgrub bya

BIBLIOGRAPHY AND ABBREVIATIONS

PRIMARY SOURCES

A – *Abhidharmakośabhāṣya of Vasubandhu*, P. Pradhan (ed.), Patna: Kashi Prasad Jayaswal Research Institute, 1967.

AS – Asaṅga, *Abhidharmasamuccaya-bhāṣyam*, N. Tatia (ed.), 2nd ed., Patna: Kashi Prasad Jayaswal Research Institute, 2005.

C – Candrakīrti, *Madhyamakāvatāra* [*dbu ma la 'jug pa*], L. de la Vallé Poussin (ed.), (Bibliotheca Buddhica 9), St. Petersbourg 1912.

D – Devendrabuddhi, *Pramāṇavārttikapañjikā* [*Tshad ma rnam 'grel gyi dka' 'grel*], D 4217 Che.

Dharmakīrti, *rgyud gzhan grub pa zhes bya ba'i rab tu byed pa*, in: *tshad ma rigs pa'i skor rgya gzhung rtsa 'grel bdam bsgrigs: deb dang po. rdo rje rgyal pos bdam bsgrigs byas pa*, Beijing: mi rigs dpe skrun khang, 1988, vol. 1.

G – Go rams pa bsod nams seng ge, *sDe bdun mdo dang bcas pa'i dgongs pa phin ci ma log par 'grel ba tshad ma rigs pa'i gter gyi don gsal bar byed pa*, in: *dpal sa skya pa'i tshad ma rig pa'i gzhung gces bsdus*, New Delhi: Institute of Tibetan Classics, 2006 (*bod kyi gtsug lag gces bdus*, vol. 20).

g.Yag ston sangs rgyas dpal, *sde bdun gyi dgongs 'grel tshad ma rigs pa'i gter gyi de kho nan yid gsal bar byed pa rigs pa'i 'od stong 'phro ba*, in: *dpal ldan sa skya pa'i gsung rab*, Beijing: mi rigs dpe skrun khang 2007, vol. tshad ma, 420–700.

Hugon P. (2002). *Le* rTags kyi rnam gzhag rigs lam gsal ba'i sgron me *de Glo bo mkhan chen bSod nams lhun grub. Un manuel tibétain d'introduction à la logique. Edition et traduction annotée*, Wien: WSTB 55.

Kamalaśīla, *Madhyamakāloka* [*dbu ma snang ba*], D 3887.

L – Glo bo mkhan chen bsod nams lhun grub, *tshad ma rigs pa'i gter 'grel pa'i rnam bshad rigs lam gsal ba'i nyi ma*, Pekin: krung go'i bod kyi shes rig dpe skrun khang, 1988.

M – 'Jam mgon 'ju mi pham rgya mtsho, in: *'jam mgon 'ju mi pham rgya mtsho'i gsung 'bum sde dge dgon chen par ma*, Paro (Bhutan): Lama Ngodrup and Sherab Drimey, 1984–1993, vol. 13.

Nāgārjuna, *Śūnyatāsaptati*, Sarnath–Varanasi: Central Institute of Higher Tibetan Studies, 1996.

PS – Dignāga, *Pramāṇasamuccaya*, D 4204.

PV – *Pramāṇavārttika*, Y. Miyasaka (ed.), *Acta Indologica*, 2, 1971–1972.

PVin – Dharmakīrti's *Pramāṇaviniścaya*, E. Steinkellner (ed.), Beijing/Vienna: China Tibetology Publishing House – Austrian Academy of Sciences Press, 2007.

rGyal tshab dar ma rin chen, *tshad ma rig pa'i gter gyi rnam bshad legs par bshad pa'i snying po*, G. Dreyfus, Sh. Onoda (eds.), Kyoto: Nagata Bunshodo, 1994.

S – Śākya mchog ldan, *Tshad ma'i mdo dang gzhung lugs sde bdun gyi de kho na nyid bsdus pa*, in: *blo gros mtha' yas pa'i mdzod*, Kathmandu: Rigpe Dorje Publications 2009, vol. 12.

S1 – Śākya mchog ldan, *tshad ma rigs gter gyi dgongs rgyan rigs pa'i 'khor los lugs ngan pham byed*, Collected Works, vol. 9, Thimpu: Kunzang Tobgey 1975.

T1 – Sa skya Paṇḍita, *Tshad ma rigs pa'i gter gyi rtsa ba dang 'grel*, Varanasi, Sarnath: Central Institute of Higher Tibetan Studies [Sakya Students' Union], 2008.

T2 – *Tshad ma rigs pa'i gter gyi rang 'brel*, in: *dpal ldan sa skya pa'i bka' bum* (reproduced from the 1736 Derge Edition), New Delhi: Sakya Center 1993, vol. 11 (*da*).

TZS – mTshur ston gZhon nu seng ge, *Tshad ma shes rab sgron ma* (2004), P. Hugon (ed.), Wien: WSTB 60.

Vetter T. (1966). Dharmakīrti's *Pramāṇaviniścaya* 1. Kapitel: *Pratyakṣam.* Einleitung, Text der tibetischen Übersetzung, Sanskritfragmente, deutsche Übersetzung, Wien: Kommissionsverlag der Osterreichischen Akademie der Wissenschaften.

SECONDARY SOURCES

Arnold D. (2005). *Buddhists, Brahmins, and Belief. Epistemology in South Asian Philosophy of Religion*, New York: Columbia University Press.

Arnold D. (2008). Buddhist Idealism, Epistemic and Otherwise. Thoughts on the Alternating Perspectives of Dharmakīrti, *Sophia*, 47(1), 3–28.

Bhattacharya R. (2012). *Svabhāvavāda* and the Cārvāka/Lokāyata: A Historical Overview, *JIP*, 40, 593–614.

bod rgya tshad ma rig pa'i tshig mdzod (1988). Beijing: People's Publication House.

Cabezón J.I., Dargyay L. (2006). *Freedom from Extremes. Go rams pa's „Distinguishing the Views" and the Polemics of Emptiness*, Boston: Wisdom Publications.

Chu J. (2006). On Dignāga's Theory of the Object of Cognition as Presented in PS(V) 1, *Journal of the International Association of Buddhist Studies*, 29(2), 211–253.

Dhammajoti K.L. (2007). *Abhidharma Doctrines and Controversies on Perception*, Hong kong: Centre of Buddhist Studies, The University of Hong Kong.

Dreyfus G.B.J. (1997). *Recognizing Reality. Dharmakīrti's Philosophy and its Tibetan Interpretations*, Delhi: Sri Satguru Publications.

Dunne J. (2004). *Foundations of Dharmakrti's Philosophy*, Boston: Wisdom Publications.

Dunne J. (2006). Realizing the Unreal: Dharmakīrti's Theory of Yogic Perception, *JIP*, 34, 497–519.

Gold J. (2007). *The Dharma's Gatekeepers: Sakya Pandita on Buddhist Scholarship in Tibet*, N.Y.: State University of New York Press.

Gold J. (2014). Sakya Paṇḍita's Anti-realism as a Return to the Mainstream, *Philosophy East & West*, 64(2), 360–374.

Horváth Z. (1984). "Structure and Content of the *Chad-ma Rigs-pa'i Gter*, an Epistemological Treatise of Sa skya Pandita", in: L. Ligeti (ed.), *Tibetan and Buddhist Studies. Commemorating the 200th Anniversary of the Birth of Alexander Csoma de Körös*, Bibliotheca Orientalis Hungarica 29(1), Budapest: Akadémiai Kiadó, 267–302.

Hugon P. (2004). Interpretations of the *trairūpya* in Tibet, *Hōrin. Vergleichende Studien zur japanischen Kultur*, 11, 95–118.

Hugon P. (2008). *Trésors du raisonnement. Sa skya Paṇḍita et ses prédécesseurs tibétains sur les modes de fonctionnement de la pensée et le fondement de l'inférence. Edition et traduction annotée du quatrième chapitre et d'une section du dixième chapitre du* Tshad ma rigs pa'i gter, Wien: WSTB 69.

Hugon P. (2012). Inherited Opponents and New Opponents: A Look at Informal Argumentation in the Tshad ma rigs gter, *Journal of Tibetology*, 8, 26–57.

Hugon P. (2011). Is Dharmakīrti Grabbing the Rabbit by the Horns? A Reassessment of the Scope of *Prameya* in Dharmakīrtian Epistemology, *JIP*, 39(4), 367–389.

Jackson D. (1987). *The Entrance Gate for the Wise (Section III). Sa-skya Paṇḍita on Indian and Tibetan Traditions of* Pramāṇa *and Philosophical Debate*, Wien: WSTB 17.

Jackson D. (1995). "The Status of Pramāna Doctrine according to Sa skya Paṇḍita and Other Tibetan Masters: Theoretical Discipline or Doctrine of Liberation?", in: T. Skorupski, U. Pagel (eds.), *The Buddhist Forum, Volume III (1991–1993). Papers in Honor and Appreciation of Professor David Seyfort Ruegg's Contribution to Indological, Buddhist and Tibetan Studies*, New Delhi: Heritage, 85–129.

JIP – Journal of Indian Philosophyi.

Kajiyama Y. (1973). Three Kinds of Affirmation and Two Kinds of Negation in Buddhist Philosophy, *Wiener Zeitschrift für die Kunde Südasiens*, 17, 161–175.

Kapstein M.T. (2000). *The Tibetan Assimilation of Buddhism. Conversion, Contestation, and Memory*, New York: Oxford University Press.

Kellner B. (2011). "Dharmakīrti's criticism of external realism and the sliding scale of analysis", in: H. Krasser, H. Lasic, E. Franco, B. Kellner (eds.), *Religion and Logic in Buddhist Philosophical Analysis. Proceedings of the Fourth International*

Dharmakīrti Conference. Vienna, August 23–27, 2005. Wien: Verlag der Österreichischen Akademie der Wissenschaften, 291–298.

Kellner B. (2014). Changing Frames in Buddhist Thought. The Concept of *Ākāra* in Abhidharma and in Buddhist Epistemological Analysis, *JIP*, 42(2–3), 275–295.

McClintock S. (2014). Kamalaśīla on the Nature of Phenomenal Content (*ākāra*) in Cognition: A Close Reading of TSP ad TS 3626 and Related Passages, *JIP*, 42(2–3), 327–337.

Moriyama S. (2014). Ratnākaraśānti's Theory of Cognition with False Mental Images (**alīkākāravāda*) and the Neither-One-Nor-Many Argument, *JIP*, 42(2–3), 339–351.

Ottmer E. (2003). *Finger, die auf den Mond zeigen: eine Gegenüberstellung europäischer und Buddhistischer Sprachtheorien am Beispiel Ferdinand de Saussures und Sakya Paṇḍitas*. Göttingen: Vandenhoeck & Ruprecht.

Perdue D.E. (1992). *Debate in Tibetan Buddhism*, New York: Snow Lion.

Pind O. (1991). "Dignāga on *śabdasāmānya* and *śabdaviśeṣa*", in: E. Steinkellner (ed.), *Studies in the Buddhist Epistemological Tradition*, Wien: Verlag der Österreichischen Akademie der Wissenschaften, 269–280.

Przybyslawski A. (2016). States of Non-cognizing Mind, in: *Tshad ma rigs gter* According to Go rams pa, *JIP*, 44, 393–410.

Rogers K.M. (2009). *Tibetan Logic*, New York: Snow Lion.

Ruegg D.S. (1994). *Pramāṇabhūta*, **Pramāṇa(bhūta)-puruṣa*, *Pratyakṣadharman* and *Sākṣātkṛtadharma* as Epithets of the *Ṛṣi*, *Ācārya* and *Tathāgata* in Grammatical, Epistemological and Madhyamaka Texts, *Bulletin of the School of Oriental and African Studies*, 57, 303–320.

Saussure F. de (1966). *Course in General Linguistics*, Ch. Bally, A. Sechehaye, A. Riedlinger; transl. (eds.), introduction and notes W. Baskin, New York–Toronto–London: McGraw-Hill Book Company.

Shaw J.L. (2002). Causality: Sāṃkhya, Bauddha, Nyāya*, *JIP*, 30, 213–270.

Silk J.A. (2002). Possible Indian Sources for the Term *tshad ma'i skyes bu* as *pramānapurura*, *JIP*, 30, 111–160.

Steinkellner E. (1977). *Verse-Index of Dharmakīrti's Works (Tibetan Versions)*, Wien: WSTB 1.

Steinkellner E. (1983). "*Tshad ma'i skyes bu*. Meaning and Historical Significance of the Term", in: E. Steinkellner, H. Tauscher (eds.), *Contributions on Tibetan Buddhist Religion and Philosophy*, Vienna: Wiener Studien zur Tibetologie, 275–284.

Stewart B.J. (2010). Sa skya Paṇḍita on the defining characteristic and variegation of direct perception (based on his *Tshad ma rigs gter* with his auto-commentary and Gorams pa's sub-commentary providing contextual and subtextual clarification), *Acta Orientalia Vilnensia*, 11(1), 53–83.

Stoltz J. (2006). Sa skya Paṇḍita and the Status of Concepts, *Philosophy East & West*, 56(4), 567–582.

Tillemans T.J.F. (1999). *Scripture, Logic, Language. Essays on Dharmakīrti and his Tibetan Successors*, Boston: Wisdom Publications.

Tillemans T.J.F. (2004). The slow death of the *trairūpya* in Buddhist Logic. A propos of Sa skya Paṇḍita, *Hōrin*, 11, 83–94.

Tola F., Dragonetti C. (1995). *On Voidness. A Study on Buddhist Nihilism*, Delhi: Motilal Banarsidass Publishers.

Tola F., Dragonetti C. (2004). *Being as Consciousness. Yogācāra Philosophy of Buddhism*, Delhi: Motilal Banarsidass Publishers.

WSTB – Wiener Studien zur Tibetologie und Buddhismuskunde, Arbeitskreis für Tibetische und Buddhistische Studien Universität Wien.

Van Bijlert V.A. (1989). *Epistemology and Spiritual Authority. The Development of Epistemology and Logic in the Old Nyāya and the Buddhist School of Epistemology with an Annotated Translation of Dharmakīrti's Pramāṇavārttika II (Pramāṇasiddhi) vv. 1–7*, Wien: WSTB 20.

Van der Kuijp L. (1979). Tibetan Contributions to the 'apoha' Theory: The Fourth Chapter of the Tshad-ma Rigs-pa'i gter, *Journal of the American Oriental Society*, 99(3), 408–422.

Van der Kuijp L.W.J. (1983). *Contributions to the Development of Tibetan Buddhist Epistemology. From the Eleventh to the Thirteenth Century*, Wiesbaden: Franz Steiner Verlag.

Van der Kuijp L.W.J. (1993a). Two Mongol Xylographs *(Hor Par Ma)* of the Tibetan Text of Sa Skya Paṇḍita's Work, *Journal of the International Association of Buddhist Studies*, 16(2), 279–298.

Van der Kuijp L.W.J. (1993b). Apropos of Some Recently Recovered Manuscripts: Anent Sa skya Paṇḍita's *Tshad ma rigs pa'i gter*, *Berliner Indologische Studien*, 7, 149–162.

Verhagen P.C. (2005). Studies in Indo-Tibetan Buddhist Hermeneutics (5). The *mkhas-pa-rnams-'jug-pa'i-sgo* by Sa-Skya Pandita kun-dga'-rgyal-mtshan", *Journal of the International Association of Buddhist Studies*, vol. 28, no. 1, 183–219.

Yao Z. (2014). "Yogācāra Critiques of the Two Truths", in: Chen-kuo Lin, M. Radich (eds.), *A Distant Mirror. Articulating Indic Ideas in Sixth and Seventh Century Chinese Buddhism*, Hamburg Buddhist Studies, 3, Hamburg: Hamburg University Press, 313–335.

Yoshimizu C. (2004). "Defining and Redefining Svalakṣaṇa: Dharmakīrti's Concept and its Tibetan Modification", in: M. Tachikawa, S. Hino, T. Wada (eds.), *Three Mountains and Seven Rivers: Prof. Musashi Tachikawa's Felicitation Volume*, Delhi: Motilal Banarsidass Publishers, 117–133.

Yoshimizu C. (2007). "Causal efficacy and spatiotemporal restriction: An analytical study of the Sautrāntika philosophy", in: B. Kellner, H. Krasser, H. Lasic, M.T. Much, H. Tauscher (eds.), *Pramāṇakīrtiḥ. Papers dedicated to Ernst Steinkellner on the occasion of his 70th birthday*, WSTB 70.2, 1049–1078.

INDEX OF NAMES

INDIAN AND TIBETAN AUTHORS

WESTERN AUTHORS

TECHNICAL EDITOR
Karolina Wąsowska

COPY EDITOR
Renata Włodek

PROOFREADER
Józefa Kunicka-Synowiec

TYPESETTER
Hanna Wiechecka

Jagiellonian University Press
Editorial Offices: Michałowskiego 9/2, 31-126 Kraków
Phone: +48 12 663 23 80, +48 12 663 23 82, Fax: +48 12 663 23 83